PLAY GOLF TO LEARN GOLF

MICHAEL HEBRON

PGA MP, CI

Science meets the art of learning golf.

When it comes to playing golf, it could be argued that technical instruction created the need for mental coaches who are telling individuals to "free up your mind and just play."

Published in 2009 by Learning Golf, Inc.,
495 Landing Avenue,
Smithtown, New York 11787
(www. michaelhebron.com)

Author: Michael P. Hebron
PGA Master Professional
PGA Certified Instructor

Library of Congress Control Number: 2008943431

ISBN 978-0-9620214-9-7
Play Golf to Learn Golf

Printed in the United States of America
by Lightning Source, Inc.
(www.lightningsource.com)

Editing by Nannette Poillon McCoy

Cover design by Martha Nichols/aMuse Productions
Book layout by Kip Williams for aMuse Productions

A Letter From Shalimi Malik

On a recent trip from my home in India to the United States I had the privilege of spending some time with Michael Hebron, the legendary teaching professional. Michael has consistently been ranked amongst the top 50 teaching professionals of the world and has won numerous awards and titles for his work including **PGA Master Professional** and **PGA Teacher of the Year**. He was the organizer of the very first PGA Teaching and Coaching Summit, and is known as the Teacher of Teachers.

Michael had graciously allowed me to come watch him teach a workshop for players of varying abilities. I took the train from Manhattan and an hour later I was sitting in Michael's car - listening to this gentle-voiced sandy-haired gentleman whose Irish blue eyes twinkle with curiosity, as he explained his ideas on golf and learning.

Michael has arrived at his method of teaching through an enormous amount of research on how the human brain works and how it learns. He had been teaching for 15 years, won a number of awards, and had people like Hank Haney say that no one knew more about the golf swing than Michael when he realized that his way of teaching wasn't getting through to everyone. His students weren't improving at the rate he believed they should have. He made a decision to change and to learn as much as he could about learning methods and how to use them.

The conclusions he arrived at are fascinating and utterly simple:

- Create a positive learning environment.
- Allow students to arrive at their own conclusions through self-discovery.
- Play to learn - not learn to play.
- Have the freedom and basic core knowledge and to be creative with what you already have instead of striving for an ideal swing.

- Stop looking at errors as negative and start treating them as useful feedback. Most importantly, to have fun with the game! Play to learn - not learn to play. In a nutshell - play it in the truest sense of the word.

I watched as Michael explained these concepts in detail to the 10 workshop golfers. Amongst them was a lady who'd never played golf before. To see her go from not knowing which way the club head should face to hitting the ball like a 18 handicapper in a few hours made me understand how little I knew about the game, and how wonderful it could be if learned in the correct way. Michael managed to make her understand what we consider complicated theories and aspects of the golf swing. She grasped the concepts of swing plane, compressing the ball, and other seemingly esoteric ideas with no difficulty. The beauty in his method of teaching (which he refers to as a learning method) is its utmost simplicity.

Michael is part of that rare breed of gentlemen. He is both generous with his time and his vast knowledge. For me personally it was a journey well worth making and I hope I get to see him again soon.

Acknowledgments

First, my thanks to all the golfers I have worked with over the years. I learned from all of them. When they were pleased with their progress, it gave me the encouragement to put my approach to paper.

I am most appreciative of the PGA of America's Education Department and the National Golf Foundation for the opportunity to give clinics and to teach all over the country. Those assignments helped develop and test my ideas.

My thanks to my fellow PGA golf professionals who took an interest and helped me grow as a person and a professional. The membership at my club, Smithtown Landing Country Club on Long Island, has always played a part in any progress I have made in golf, and this book must be included. I want to thank my friends and family. A special thank you to GB,GB for support over the years.

A special thanks to members of my staff from over the years, Rick Neilson, Maureen Fisher, Valerie Flora, Douglas Breuer, Tim Horan, Henry Kilroy, and especially my son Michael. Without their help this book would not have been possible. I also want to thank Nannette Poillon McCoy, Ryan Hayden and others who have contributed to the revisions and the translations.

Michael Hebron
PGA MP CI

SWING SHIFT:
PRO PUSHES BETTER WAY OF LEARNING

Port St. Lucie, Florida: The future of golf instruction might come from lessons from the past when Michael Hebron delivers his message to the professionals gathering at the PGA Teaching and Coaching Summit this weekend. Hebron, a former PGA Teacher of the Year who has written many books about golf instruction, helped organize the first summit back in 1988. Since then his ideas on instruction have changed dramatically. His newest book, *Play Golf to Learn Golf*, emphasizes the learning process.

"Technology has done a lot for golf." Hebron said. "It has improved the ball, it has improved the club, it has even improved the grass we play on." But some technology, such as the emphasis on electronic swing analysis, where we break down every movement of every player's swing and try to make it perfect, is not helping people learn. The brain doesn't learn that way. We learn through guided experimenting and self assessment."

"For 20 years I have taught the wrong way." Hebron said Thursday at the PGA Learning Center. "I knew lots about the golf swing but I didn't know anything about how people learn."

"There are only a few things that you have to do when you are hitting a golf ball." he said. "You have to swing the club on plane through impact, and you have to swing the club so the shaft reaches impact before the clubface because that's the way the club has been designed to work."

Hebron's new lessons are consistent with principles that famous touring pros Jack Nicklaus and Lee Trevino followed to Hall of Fame careers.

Nicklaus believed the swing is a simple process. Trevino has long believed players must use the club as it is designed to be used. The question is why golf instruction progressed only to get to a point where one basic swing is etched in stone and its parts became more important than the whole.

Hebron believes instruction should emphasize developing workable habits and avoid trying to fix poor habits. He believes that bad swings aren't all bad because they serve as a guide to lead a player to a different swing with more desirable results.

Hebron said, "We're hoping this is a paradigm shift in teaching that is back to how we're supposed to learn."

*Jerry Potter in **USA TODAY**, December 5, 2008*

Michael Hebron's opening remarks at the 2008 PGA of America Teaching and Coaching Summit

As golf professionals we are to be ambassadors for this great game. In the future our PGA call letters could stand for **P**leasurable **G**ame for **A**ll. Golf is a frustrating game to many who are playing, and to the many that stop playing every year. Hopefully, what follows can benefit PGA members and our association's efforts to grow the game.

We are not going to debate the value of one swing theory over another. As the famous English golf instructor, John Jacobs, said, "There is some good in every golf book - its value depends on the reader's point of view." What follows travels through studies into brain compatible approaches to learning and teaching. Why should we care about the brain? Because it runs the show. The brain is the gateway to learning, higher order thinking, seeing options, and problem solving skills. "Improvement begins in the brain for everyone." - Dr. Ken Gibson.

The brain has an internal information processing system. When learning, to gain the highest return on the investment of time and resources, any information-delivery system must be compatible with the brain's processing system. Approaches to functional development do not pit the internal working of the brain and the external operations of the body against each other. It is only after the brain changes that there can be a physical change in the way we move.

I have never seen myself as a perfect teacher, but I have learned that there are perfect learners and they are called human beings. This was an insight I did not have for the first 20 years as a PGA instructor. Back then, it could be said that I was teaching with a "B" game approach. Today, with the help of award-winning educators and scientists and their research, I am doing my best to move in the direction of developing an "A" game approach for helping people learn.

This presentation is a cautious and modest effort to share insights that may seem counter intuitive and clearly non-traditional. When I became aware of insights into the biological and dynamic nature of learning, I had to keep an open mind. I suggest everyone here today do the same.

For example, studies show that drills, TV replay, expert models, detailed information, acts of fixing, are all less useful than I once thought them to be.

The reality is that there are more individuals in schools, business training, and sports instruction who do not reach their potential than those who do. This truth has caused some rethinking. During the 1990s and beyond, modern science has been uncovering more about the nature of learning than at any other time in the history of research. These are realities about acts of learning that I never imagined existed for the first twenty years I was teaching. Today, the 1990s are called "the decade of the brain."

This presentation is not a sales pitch or a live infomercial. It is not an effort to prove or disprove anything.

But, I will say this presentation is based on sound science for use in the 21st century in classrooms, business training, and on sports practice fields. This research suggests using an approach to learning that gives individuals choices and general 'just in the ballpark' concepts. No details – no fixing needed.

- How do we go from not knowing to knowing?
- How did lessons provided become lessons learning?
- Is the approach to teaching and learning brain compatible?

An efficient approach to learning shines a light; it is not trying to get something right. Fixing isn't learning.

What ever I know, or have been given credit for knowing, is much less than what there is to know. As Mark Twain wrote, "The difficulty ain't that we know so much, but that we know so much that ain't so."

Play with the idea that students who are not learning don't need more education, it's the approach to learning that needs some rethinking, and more education.

I respectively suggest that this presentation about the nature of learning and the brain will be the most valuable presentation at this summit. Why? Because how could any approach to teaching expect to reach its potential without first taking into consideration the very nature of learning information and skills? There are cognitive skills, sports skills, and academic skills. It is the quality of cognitive skills that influences the quality of all other skills.

A master of anything was first a master of learning.

If the value of this topic does not become apparent here today, sparking more interest about teaching with the brain in mind, it is a weakness in this presentation and not the value of the research, and I apologize.

As James E. Zull, director of the University Center for Innovation in Teaching said,

"Now that we are finding out how the brain works, it is now possible to have teaching approaches that can dramatically improve human learning."

Whether or not teachers inform themselves and make the effort to discover and use this new research, cognitive science will continue to make valuable discoveries about acts of learning and teaching at an ever-increasing pace.

What a tragedy it would be if teachers of any topic, including golf, choose to remain uninformed about this historic paradigm shift that approaches to learning are currently using in schools, business, and many sports all over the world.

According to research from modern science, to reach our potential as a golf instructor, it helps to mix insights about a golf swing and playing a game with accurate insights into the nature of learning and teaching (with the brain in mind.)

Self-modification is the principle activity of the brain. But, the brain does not look for an exact selection. Allowing a natural drift through self-organization and self-assessment that experiences both workable and unworkable outcomes. During playful acts of learning the brain uses both workable and unworkable outcomes to change itself.

Opportunities now exist for students and teachers to have strong scientific support for developing brain compatible information delivery systems.

I now realize that every golfer who makes the choice to spend time with any teacher is a perfect learner. These students are not broken or in need of having their golf swing fixed. These individuals are not hard-wired to miss putts, make poor decisions, or fail tests in school.

Efficient approaches to learning see students as lights that are already burning bright and they are just helping students to teach themselves to burn even brighter.

Efficient approaches to learning help golfers to invent their own golf swing, putting stoke, and tempo! Efficient approaches to progress are missionaries for learning, not teachers of subjects.

Studies show that these new insights into the nature of learning can enhance every instructor's approach and every golfer's ability to learn and enjoy golf.

Individuals learn faster and retain information longer when information delivery systems are brain compatible. By moving beyond what goes on outside the brain (the golf swing) to include the inner workings of the brain (where the golf swing has its origin), learning becomes less frustrating. Play with the ideas that what makes a golf swing work can't be filmed and information that is geared for helping someone is not as useful as information that is geared for helping them help themselves. You can't film the brain's creative process!

Throughout this summit, keep in mind that information does not produce good learning, anymore than paint produces good art. Information can be interesting, but at the same time educationally vacant.

When learning is brain compatible it is a playful active process, guided by the best ingredients on earth: acts of curiosity, imagination, and random improvisation. We all clearly play to learn, we do not have to learn how to play.

It is brain-on, hands-on entertainment when learning is efficient – making golf a **pleasurable game for all**!

Michael Hebron's School for Learning Golf
Learning Golf Workshops, Seminars, Speaking Engagements, and Lessons
800-444-0565 or 631-979-6534
www.michaelhebron.com
email michael@michaelhebron.com

Other Books by Michael Hebron

See and Feel the Inside Move the Outside
Building and Improving Your Golf Mind, Golf Body, Golf Swing
Golf Swing Secrets and Lies, Six Timeless Lessons
The Art and Zen of Learning Golf

DVDs

Blueprints for Learning Golf
Blueprints for Parents and Children Learning Golf (English and French)
Building and Improving Your Golf Mind, Golf Body, Golf Swing

A Letter from Mary Walsh, Washington, DC

My First Golf Swing (A Testament to Playful Learning!)

I see golf as an exacting sport - small ball, small hole, minute errors producing catastrophic results. I know this from watching golf on TV and movies like *Tin Cup*.

So my goals for this first lesson were precise - I would present well and become putty to be shaped into perfection by my teacher.

Now that I've met Michael Hebron, I think I'll drop the word teacher. Sensei is better, "knowledgeable one," "someone who has achieved a certain level of mastery in an art form." Yes, that would be Michael.

He didn't see me as putty. There was no introduction into how to hold the club, no shaking hands with the racket, as in tennis. My rough idea of a grip seemed good enough; he gave me no precise instruction on where to place my feet, no technical advice on how to address the ball.

Michael suggested a putt-putt swing - oh yeah baby; now I can relax! - then swinging with one hand. Finally, I hit two handed. It seemed to be going well.

Swing with your shoulders, not your wrists, he said. We circulated my wrists to loosen them up, keep them free. Winding up for the swing, yes, **it's OK**, bend your elbows - that's what they want to do anyway. Following through - another good thing. Every suggestion made the movement more natural. Yes, lift your foot to help with the follow through, much better.

All the iron-clad rules I had been expecting melted away. No dos and don'ts. Was my sensei teaching me and I didn't even notice?

I came to this lesson wanting no less than joy - the joy of a well-hit ball. I came away with something else - delight. Michael didn't teach me to hit the ball; he sort of let me hit it. I was digging into myself to find how.

Not every ball was a winner, but some were pretty darn good. In my mind it went like this: Relax. Let it go, let it go - just swing and follow through.

When it sailed up and out beautifully I knew delight. Michael was pleased. He called a class of children over to witness the progress of a real live first time golfer. No pressure there, just twenty pairs of young eyes, little golfers better than me.

My sensei says that golf is about two things - distance and direction. To that I would add delight.

Table of Contents

Suggested Mission Statement for Efficient Learning Environments

- Promote self-reliance.
- Strive for personal growth.
- Honor each individual and their choices.
- Encourage curiosity and imagination.
- Support self-understanding and self-esteem.
- Support self-development, self-organization, self-discovery.
- Avoid judgments and corrections.
- Provide a positive environment.
- Enhance what already works.
- Improve observation skills.
- Uncover ordinary things that produce extraordinary results.
- Try for excellence with what you have, and what you have improves.

One goal of education is to make learning enjoyable. Students in S.A.F.E. learning-developing environments (free of judgments and criticisms) will move forward, evaluating the experience after it happens. On the other hand, in unsafe teaching fixing-to-get-it-right environments, students have concerns before they act. Efficient learning environments motivate individuals toward higher-order thinking that is conducive to creativity, in fail-free conditions, producing unforgettable learning.

Dedication

The sport, game, and business of golf have two important groups, amateurs and professionals. Amateurs are mentioned first because they are the game's first players and they have been the soul of the game from its inception. Without amateurs, the sport would not have professionals.

We could say, in some ways amateurs are the heartbeat of the game. They purchase greens fees, pay membership dues, and buy golf equipment, accessories, and golf lessons. Amateurs travel on golf vacations, are members of golf leagues, and are on the committees that govern play. Amateurs also volunteer their time to run many tournaments that raise money for charities.

Amateur golfers all over the world are the game, and this book was written with them in mind.

It was also written for professionals who support the amateurs' efforts to enjoy their participation in golf at every level, while fostering respect for the game's history and traditions. As the game of golf grows and welcomes new golfers, its values and traditions should not be left behind. I dedicate what follows to growing the game of golf through ways that may seem counter-intuitive.

What has been compiled here is grounded in realities from the Nature of Learning that can guide individuals in the direction of developing skills that are personal in nature. Meaningful, relevant, and worthwhile insights into productive approaches to learning that respected research has demonstrated accelerates progress follows.

I have never seen myself as a perfect teacher, but with the help of award winning cognitive scientists I have learned there are perfect learners and they are called human beings who have always played to learn.

- **Play** never tries to memorize - but has wonderful long-term memory.
- **Play** never has failure, only feedback that's never wrong.
- **Play** does not rely on directions, but always gets to its destination.
- **Play** tries what's new and different, and has little fear.
- **Play** takes risks (learning requires risks) but is never anxious.
- **Play** has many *Ah!* moments that last forever.
- **Play** happens in safe environments. (Learning requires a safe environment where outcomes are not being corrected by others).
- **Play** does not try to be exact, but often is.

Advancing a potential for learning requires insights into supporting the dignity of the individual student. *Enhancing such dignity improves the influence individuals will have over their own life.* America was to be the land of a free and independent will, where one could accomplish their own visions. When organized formal approaches to education started to use controlling acts of teaching, this often birthed non-thinking students who no longer felt free to explore, discover, and invent. Free will allows individuals to invest in themselves, as they gain an education that is useful in ever-changing real world environments. This kind of education cannot be given, but it can be gained through the free will of using self-skills including, self-discovery and self-assessment. Freedom in all its facets preserves the very foundation upon which curiosity, observations, and learning are set. Relevant learning, meaningful progress, and long term development support the dignity of a human being's self-image and grows their self-reliance skills. This is not a new reality, but only a return to what has always existed at the core of fully experiencing what it means to be a human being, and not a human follower.

Fearless Learning

Approaches to learning and progress are efficient when they rid individuals of fear, which is toxic to learning. The authentic soul of learning develops fearless students. It's fear, not a lack of information or skills, that is the enemy of learning. Let me introduce you to a new phrase, *"Learning-developing approach to progress."* This concept encompasses the belief that both *workable* and *unworkable* results are of equal value during playful fearless learning. A learning-developing approach to progress roots out the fear of having our orthodox method challenged and our poor habits exposed.

Unfortunately, eager learners are often poorly served by technical approaches to fixing habits. Technical approaches to fixing habits can lead us away from the inner power of play and self-discovery.

When we decide to change something, we are on a journey of discovery. Where we must go is always changing, therefore approaches to progress should develop a tool box of skills and ideas to play with, not a map to follow. Memory of workable and unworkable results can also be stored in this tool box for future reference.

Efficient approaches to learning direct our attention to acts of play. There is **P**owerful **L**earning **A**bout **Y**ourself© in acts of play that is free from the fear and stress that following how-to directions can create. The very nature of playing to learn uses a language **that does not increase anxiety while fostering acts of curiosity.**

The suggestion here is play to learn. Take in ***results*** on a journey where all that occurs (workable and unworkable) is a part of the experience. Whatever I know, or have been given credit for knowing, is much less than what there is to know.

Foreword

The Good News: Modern science has uncovered previously unknown insights into the nature of the learning process that allows individuals to have more influence over their own pace of progress when they are learning anything, even golf.

The Bad News: Most individuals are unaware of this research into how they can enhance their ability to learn.

The views and research presented in this book put a light on the ***nature of learning*** and ***brain-compatible learning*** principles. This book mixes basic core information about the golf swing and playing golf with insights into how human beings learn and how we go from not knowing to knowing. What follows suggests a self-discovery approach to progress, grounded in natural curiosity, that can grow personal insights. Personal insights have been found to be more valuable for long-term learning than following a list of details, even if it is from a perceived expert.

The central theme of what is presented here in *Play Golf to Learn Golf* is the notion that when acts of learning anything (even golf) are efficient, *they are more about playing-to-learn, than learning-to-play.* While this may seem like a counter-intuitive view, it's supported by years of research from modern science into brain compatible learning principles. These brain principles are the building blocks for making progress.

As I became more interested in golf instruction, I was also curious about how to improve someone's ability to learn the game. After I started a journey in this direction I soon discovered that there was a difference between trying to help a golf swing and trying to help a golfer. Remember the old adage, "Give a man a fish and he'll eat for a day; teach a man to fish and he can feed himself for a lifetime." **When you try to help a golf swing, unfortunately, you can win or lose, but when you help a golfer you always win!**

Perhaps the instruction industry should be seen as caretakers of a pleasurable game, not teachers of swings. Trying to teach is different from helping someone learn. What I refer to as *learning-developing environments* have been found to be more efficient for making progress than *teaching-fixing to get-it-right environments* which are self-limiting.

Golf instruction has been on a dynamic and ever changing journey that has offered up countless theories since at least 1857. This was the year *The Golfer's Manual*, considered golf's first instruction book, was published. For over 150 years most instruction offerings have read like the authors believed they had found something unknown about the golf swing, some new truth, turning a corner that no one else could see. Yes, perceived experts all, including myself at times. Hopefully, I have moved on by gaining insights into the nature of learning and efficient information delivery systems.

Many golf books seem to be trying to wring out every detailed description they could from the motions of a golfer's body and golf club. It is as if these many details are dusted with magic that was going to make swinging the club and playing the game easier. It could seem like these books were in constant competition with each other, seeking to crack some perceived secret about the art of playing golf. At the same time there is little or no mention about the nature of learning in these books filled with details and how-to directions.

Play Golf to Learn Golf was written to help people discover **they can learn to make progress without how-to advice from perceived experts** or excessive trying. Hopefully, every golfer's self-esteem will soar as they are reminded that **playful learning and growth through playful self-discovery are pleasurable and natural, proactive experiences**.

When a learner's self-discovery efforts are **encouraged** and **supported** by advice givers who avoid how-to advice, our earliest motion patterns (both sound and unsound) can plant the seeds of progress. This book is dedicated to helping reader's (both advice receivers and givers) discover their possibilities for growth through **growth-oriented choices**. Learning changes behavior. Changing behavior has always happened through playful self-discovery. Studies show that when the opportunity to integrate playful self-discovery is overlooked, learning can be incomplete or fragmented.

The culture of golf is often divided by **"low"** and **"high"** handicaps. In this culture there are people who can and people who cannot play what they themselves believe to be good golf. Unfortunately, in a can and cannot culture, everything is set up for people to believe that their lack of progress is because of their own shortcomings and they start looking for more how-to advice. Individuals rarely evaluate how they have been trying to learn. **"How useful is my current approach to learning the game?" "Should I be using a different approach?"** Probably yes is the view here.

Jeff Silverman said, "Golf is a game that is often divided against its self." For example, golf is fun to play, but can be seen as not much fun to learn. He went on to say, "If we do not know who we are as golfers, and what connects us to the game, we are not much more than the penciled in numbers on one's score card." **Golf should not be reduced to a mere number on a score card.** If golfers are going to experience the joy of personal progress, the pleasure of playing golf must be more significant than the pursuit of perfection. The pure pleasure of learning and playing a game should be an ongoing experience.

Today it seems the present culture of the golf industry is sidestepping the pleasure of playing a game by promoting perfection (i.e., the perfect swing, the perfect ball, the perfect club). When trying for perfection, frustration becomes the end product. The call letters of the PGA of America could stand for a **P**leasurable **G**ame for **A**ll.[1] When trying for perfection, frustration becomes the end product. Progress arrives through the pleasure of playing golf with self-discovery, self-assessment, and self-reliance as members of your foursome!

I have had the pleasure of being involved with golf instruction for over 40 years. I have visited more than 30 PGA sections in the United States, traveling to Europe, Asia, Canada, Bermuda, and South America hopefully helping people learn this game we care so much for.

Every student (junior, men, women, teaching, and touring professionals) has helped me make progress with my profession. But my ability to communicate instruction information was enhanced after becoming aware of the information you are about to read. I trust it will be as useful to you as it has been to students and to me. **I have come to realize that golf is a game to be played, not a subject to be taught.**

The skills of playing are learned through acts of playing. We learn about cooking when we are cooking, we are learning about skiing when we are skiing, we should play golf to learn about playing golf. This is a view that many golfers overlook in favor of following how-to directions from a perceived expert. ***We are human beings, not human followers.*** When we change the way we look at things, what we see changes. By seeing the value of playing to learn, our ability to make progress is enhanced. Playful participation avoids how-to directions. Playful participation with basic core knowledge is at the core of long term progress.

What approach to learning can help to transform information from books, magazines, teachers, experiences, etc., into personally usable, real world knowledge or know-how? Some research points to the "genius of play," or "the intelligence of play" (a Chuck Hogan term); which is at the core of integrative critical thinking and developmental learning. For example, for making progress in golf it is more useful to playfully try different ball locations in the stance, or different tempos,

1 **P**leasurable **G**ame for **A**ll is a trademark of Learning Golf Inc.

or different grip pressure, or different weight distribution, than trying to get-it-right by following how-to directions from a perceived expert.

The topic of learning has several components; information, explanations, and demonstrations are some obvious components, as is our memory. Other components include:

(1) the approach that is being used to deliver information,

(2) how individuals are being asked to learn, and

(3) past experiences.

These three components have a profound influence on the speed and quality of learning and on our ability to recall information in school, business, and sports instruction.

After spending time in teaching-fixing to-get-it-right environments, when asked what they learned many golfers will answer they learned, "I have a bad swing," "I can't putt," "I have poor alignment," "I have so much to think about." Students in schools will often answer they learned, "I can't spell," and "I am bad at math," or "I can't read." These information delivering systems have a negative approach to progress that overlooks the elements that make up what the science of learning would define as a "proactive learning experience."

A Disadvantage?

Without consciously trying to get something right, unconscious, intuitive, and spontaneous acts of playing to learn can lead us in the direction of reaching our potential. Perhaps when it comes to "letting it go" without conscious thinking golfers may be at a disadvantage. When playing tennis, baseball, or basketball there is only a short time span between each tennis return, each pitch and swing, or the act of shooting after receiving the basketball, compared to how much time golfers have in between each swing. Golfers often have five or more minutes between swings. When not playing up to their potential many golfers use the time between swings to consciously judge what went wrong, thinking about the details of the golf swing, or how they should fix an unwanted outcome; all of which can fragment one's ability to "let it go" and just play golf.

When playing 18 holes golfers are on the golf course for four hours or more. When shooting a score of, let's say 100, golfers would only be swinging their golf club for less than 200 seconds. During the time between golf swings any conscious thinking about swing theory, or how to move one's body is not as useful as staying engaged with the present and allowing a general *feel* and a general *visualization* of what one wants to do with the golf club (based on past experiences) unconsciously guide the next swing. US Olympic champion diver, Laura Wilkson said, "Once you get to the end of the platform your body knows what to do - there is no thinking."

The opinion here is that it is more useful to pretend and imagine you're swinging a club like a Jack Nicklaus, Annika Sorenstam, Tiger Woods, Lorena Ochoa, or a Ben Hogan, than trying to exactly copy computer models of their swings. This view is also shared by the Sciences of Learning as well.

Both young and adult golfers who are participating in a golf learning environment that is grounded in technical information about the golf swing and playing the game are not experiencing a brain compatible approach to progress. The value of promoting child-like imagination, and the fantasy of pretending to be who you want to be like is being side-stepped in favor of teaching-fixing to get-it-right approaches (like a computer printout) that are not compatible with the nature of the learning process. **Accurate information is only one side of the story. The nature of the learning process and the transfer of information is the other side.** Efficient approaches to learning are also efficient approaches for remembering.

What has been compiled here shows how acts of playing can enhance learning golf (or anything), relative to insights from cognitive science and their underpinning. **"Meaningful learning involves acknowledging the brain's rules for learning and teaching, and keeping those rules in mind."**[2] The nature of brain-compatible learning principles transcends both partisan descriptions of content

2 Caine and Caine, *Making Connections,* pg 4

that are always changing, and many traditional approaches to progress.

I am sure all golfers would like to feel they could improve their level of play. Instruction information can provide several different choices when a golfer is looking for help but very few of those approaches take the nature of the learning process into consideration. Any approach to instruction that is not improving the way a student plays, or their enjoyment of the game, is instruction that is going in the wrong direction, or instruction that is misunderstood.

The view here is that golf, or any motor skill, really cannot be taught, but can be learned. Every student learns in his or her own best way and at a different pace. The point here is that ***we play to learn***, we do not have to learn to play.

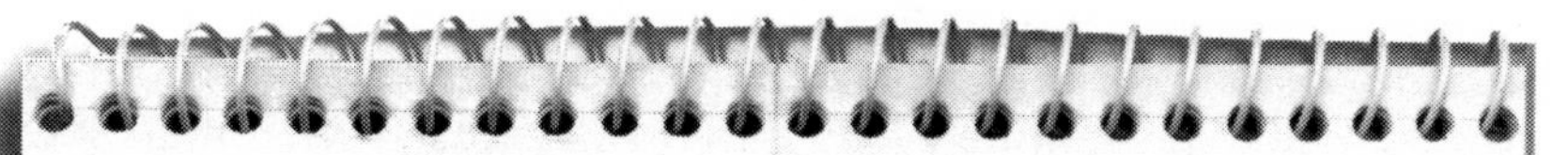

Note: Normally when I ask someone to put all they know about what they do for a living in a box — then tell me how much of that knowledge was taught to them and how much of it they learned, the typical answer is 10% taught and 90% learned.

In playing-to-learn environments students are being guided in the direction of reaching their optimal potential with general (just in the ball park) concepts, free of technical details. The brain does not encode details; it encodes and uses patterns and relationships. Playing-to-learn environments help individuals to invent skills that are personal in nature. "I am here to help you invent your way of putting, swinging, or holding the club" is the aim of playing-to-learn golf environments.

The human race has always played to learn, we did not have to learn how to play. Golfers who are not pleased with their pace of progress should consider a play-to-learn approach to progress that is grounded in self-determination and novel diversity. I refer to playing-to-learn environments as "learning-developing" environments, and learning-to-play environments as "teaching-fixing to get-it-right" environments that merely see students as objects to be fixed.

"Learning-developing" environments support growth, "teaching-fixing to get it right" environments try to manage failure.

In my view, one of the main reasons some golfers are not happy with their level of play is because of how they are trying or are asked to learn. Unsound approaches to the learning process puts limits on the progress that could be made with any physical activity.

Suggestions and information here in *Play Golf to Learn Golf* come from many sources, including my previous books. Information about the Genius of Play, Development of Physical Activities, The Discipline of Zen, Mind Sets for Progress, Attention, and Awareness, follow with the hope that readers can develop personal insights into making progress with their golf game.

I became aware of what is commonly known as the Eastern or Asian approaches to learning while flying to the 1982 Ladies U.S. Open in California. I was accompanying Anne Heuschneider, a 19-year-old who had qualified for this prestigious tournament after playing golf for only 3 years. At the time I may have been more excited than she was. Anne really had no idea how much she had accomplished in such a short period of time.

During our flight we were drawn into a conversation with a man who was in the recording business, producing records in Los Angeles and New York. When Mr. Wear discovered we were on our way to the Ladies U.S. Open, he wanted to know how or why Anne improved so quickly. First, I pointed out that Anne had put 6 or 7 years of work into 3 years, and that I believe that "Golf really cannot be taught, but it can be learned through acts of play."

After explaining my approach to instruction, Mr. Wear suggested I read a few books about the Zen approach to learning. He felt this was similar to the one I was using with students.

I took his suggestions to heart and set out to discover everything possible about the Eastern or Asian approach to learning and how it could improve my ability as an instructor and the golf skills of students. I had done some reading about Zen in the past and was excited about starting again. I would soon learn that the concept of instructors learning from lessons as well as learning from their students was basic to all efficient instruction and making progress.

Perhaps this is the reason practice halls in the Far East are traditionally called "The Place of Enlightenment" (DOJO in Japan, DQJANG in Korea, and KWOON in China). The DOJO (or Place of Enlightenment) is where we make contact with fears - anxieties - reactions - our habits and ourselves. It is where the opponent is not an opponent but a partner engaged in helping us understand ourselves more fully. A DOJO can be any place where a source of self-enlightenment is available and progress occurs through acts of play. Many golfers who want to improve often overlook the *genius of play* in favor of focusing on technical information about the golf swing, and details about moving their bodies.

I use **bold print**, quotes and *italics* throughout this book to encourage readers to "think a bit." My intent is for readers to draw their own personal meanings from the quotes. If you do not ponder what is presented here, this book is less useful than it's intended it to be. To be informed is not enough when trying to improve. Information must be experienced and personalized if you are going to learn from it. I hope some of these quotes give you new insights, and lead to new ideas that open your own pathway to progress. The quoted phrases may give you a different way of looking at yourself and your golf. The **bold print**, quotes and *italics* are meant to be embellished and expanded, to cause a bigger and clearer personal picture to learn from.

This book does not make suggestions on how to play golf, but it makes some suggestions about playfully learning and improving your golf game. Any golfer, from beginner to professional, can use this information. *Play Golf to Learn Golf* is less about the skills that you use to play golf with, than how you are trying to learn them.

Some points that will be highlighted:

- Learning golf is a creative, playful process.
- Golf is not a subject; it is a physical activity or motor skill.
- Physical activities are created in the brain, not by the body.

- Everyone learns in his or her own best way and at a different pace.
- Unfortunately, most of us have been ingrained with the Puritan work ethic: "If you don't try hard, you will not succeed."

Hopefully you will come to understand that the very act of trying brings tension and rigidity. Once we understand how we learn through playing, we will stop trying.

T R Y could stand for the mnemonic:

Talking and
Ridiculing
Yourself when learning.

Denise McCluggage's book, *The Centered Skier*, gave me some wonderful insights into the thinking process and learning. The following came from notes I made from this must read book. In it, Denise may have given the best description of the golf swing I have ever heard or read, **"The swing is an action in which certain things are caused to happen and certain things are allowed to happen. Faults arise in trying to cause what should be allowed."**

When we go to school or take lessons to *get* something, we tend to look upon learning as acquisition, adding to an existing fund of knowledge just as we would add to a bookshelf. Thus, we put ourselves under the tension of searching out and adding to our knowledge. Our brow furrows, our neck tenses, and we direct our fierce attention outward, ever fearful of missing something. And thus we do miss it; for what we are looking for is not outside; it is inside, awaiting self-discovery, awaiting awakening, awaiting the spark that is based on our past experiences.

Playful learning is not adding on; it is paring down. It is replacing old patterns; it is recording and reconnecting. Most efficient learning is replacing a complicated, less complete way with a simpler, more encompassing way. **It is seeing the picture as a whole.** At an early age we know everything we need to know. Learning stems from what happens when I do this or don't do that. Playful learning merely brings awareness. Learning does not stem from do this or don't do that. Learning happens when you notice what happens as you playfully move in different ways. If you like what happens then continue to do what you did. Attend to the process and the desired result will follow like grass grows. See it. Feel it. Avoid using words as you play to learn.

Teaching-fixing environments can destroy most of the intuitive and creative capacity of individuals by the things we say or make them do. **We destroy this capacity by making them afraid; afraid of not doing what other people want, or not pleasing, of making mistakes, of failing, of being wrong.** Thus, we make them afraid to gamble, afraid to experiment, afraid to try the difficult and unknown. (There is no failure, only usable feedback when playing to learn.)

We use physical, emotional, and intellectual functions. The important thing to remember about these three functions is that we do have a choice about the way we employ them. **The most fundamental misuse is the failure to make choices.** The body is our instrument for fulfilling our purpose on earth. This instrument can be coarse and dull in a teaching environment or tuned and receptive in learning environments - the choice is ours. Most problems are the result of conflict; our bodies tell us one thing, our thoughts another and our emotions yet another. **In most people the idea "Am I right?" seems to be associated with a fixed pattern of tension that prevents experiencing a new and freer balance.** At the risk of feeling disoriented, trust, venturing from the known to the unknown. This journey necessitates a willingness both to make mistakes and to profit by them. Feedback from play is the essence of progress.

The last chapter of the book is called **Extra Credit**. Reading this chapter is similar to extra credit work in classroom settings. It contains details that may interest some readers but it is information that can be used by every reader.

CHAPTER ONE
Rethinking Acts of Learning and Teaching

The text in this book represents a composite of views from the sciences of learning. Hopefully, what follows will empower both givers and receivers of information with a fluid document of insights into the nature of learning and genius of play. This book is intended to be a proactive, optimistic presentation that hopefully will be an effective tool for enhancing acts of learning golf or anything.

Today there are many approaches to learning embedded with tradition, but we are learning from science that some implicitly accepted traditional teaching practices are not helping with skill acquisition. **The unfortunate reality is that there are many more individuals in all walks of life who don't reach their potential than do. Learning involves a transfer of information, which cognitive science suggests occurs in counter-intuitive ways and not as tradition often expects it will.**

After exploring research on the nature of the learning process, I have compiled information about human development here that is consistent with the indirect preparation gained from an individual's past experiences.

Efficient learning is based more on the design of the information delivery system that is being used, than the information being shared. How new information is delivered to a receiver, and then the receiver to themselves, should be compatible with how the brain normally learns. Often it is not a lack of talent, but how individuals approach learning that can fragment progress.

Belief systems about learning often need some rethinking. "To more fully use the brain's capacity to learn we must grasp the elegance of the way the brain learns."[3] The brain is our gateway to learning and approaches to progress that expect to be efficient should take this reality into consideration. **When viewed through acts of play, there is a dramatic change in the way we understand how we best learn.** In his book, *How Tiger Does It*, Brad Kearns says, "Tiger Woods approaches golf with the youthful innocence of a child at play." (pg 49)

If the aim of the game of golf is playing golf, it therefore seems logical that progress with golf would come from a playing-to-learn approach. Said another way, if playing golf is the aim, let's begin with the end product - playing.

Concerns and questions about a lack of progress, poor outcomes or bad habits tend to be personal in nature. There would be a greater impact on making progress if questions such as, "Why is this taking me so long?" or, "Why am I not getting this?" were focused on the design of approach to learning being used. When people are not making progress they tend to look for the next tip, or a different source of information. I suggest that it would be more productive for them to ask if there is a different way to learn what they are trying to accomplish. **Yes there is, would be the response here.**

Acts of efficient learning, or how one actually goes from not knowing to knowing is a topic that has transfixed me since the mid 1980s. It was an eye opening experience for me to learn "the process of change is random."[4] For someone who had received awards for their work as a teacher while using a long list of details and technical information (for 20 years) the reality that learning is mostly random was more than eye opening, it was liberating. The insight that learning is random

---

3 Caine and Caine, *Making Connections*, pg 23

4 Bill Bryson, *A Short History of Nearly Everything*, pg 3

changed how I approached instruction and has guided my thinking since the late 1980s.

Two examples of random learning come from Ben Hogan and Tiger Woods: Tiger Woods only talks about enhancing his game, not fixing it. His curiosity creates a positive approach to playful experimenting. Ben Hogan said, "I experimented, I learned by trial and error [I would say trial and *feedback*] experimenting continually with new ideas, adopting and refining."

"Just fool around and play with it, and you will learn to do it just fine." Keep that often used statement in mind as you read on. Acts of play let curiosity, self-assessment, and self-discovery take the lead. True play permissibly breaks some rules letting spontaneity and creativity travel into the process of learning, going beyond a narrow focus on right or wrong outcomes. It's by playfully walking a tightrope that you can capture the balance of personal progress and long term learning. The will to succeed is important, but the will to go through the process of learning is vital.

Martha Kaufeldt, award winning educator, said in her book *Begin with the Brain*, "Encourage creative thinking, inventiveness, and playfulness." The problem solving brain has a playing, exploring, and curious mindful approach to progress. The problem is not the problem, it is the approach to the problem that is often the problem when progress is slow.

Playing golf is a physical, mental, and emotional process. While these elements of playing golf are normally recognized, acts of playing golf are often taken for granted and not seen for their full and far-reaching developmental value. **Insights into how acts of playing will help you learn golf are valuable for making progress.** A view supported by cognitive science is that we should clearly be playing-to-learn, and not trying to learn how to play. Play-to-learn environments combine brain storming options with confidence and joy.

Webster's Dictionary defines "play" in several ways:

(1) To act in a way that seems OK while it is developing, rather than acting in accordance with a plan.

(2) To give full play to ones imagination.

(3) To operate over a broad area.

(4) To use various ways.

Keep these views of play in mind as you read on, especially number one. The genius of true play allows non-competitive self-discovery to form deeper learning than competitive "get-it-right" acts that leave individuals with a limited view of what playing-to-learn can accomplish. "When Tiger was playing he had the ability to forget bad shots." (Rudy Duran)

It's accurate to say that what has been compiled herein has taken a lifetime of experiences to gather. Insights gained from others and their research has also touched and runs deep into what has been put to paper herein. Hopefully, what has been put forward will not be seen as mis-speaking, or be misunderstood, because it is counter-intuitive and filled with rare truths about learning. Again, I have never seen myself as a perfect teacher, but I have learned from award winning cognitive scientists that there are perfect learners and they are called human beings who play to learn! The human race, you and I, were designed to develop, thrive, and succeed; not to fail. We were not designed to miss putts, make poor business decisions, or fail tests in school. We were designed to learn without consciously trying to learn, in safe non-judgmental environments. The seeds of progress are watered by self-discovery and self-assessment, avoiding the blind spots that following directions can cause.

We are designed to learn first, then teach ourselves to use what we have learned. After we learn something is dangerous, we teach ourselves to avoid or combat it. Unfortunately, some approaches to progress are trying to teach first.

CHAPTER TWO
The Genius of Play

Let's play with the idea that from the day we are born, and for every day of our lives, we have all played to learn, and unconsciously developed, and made progress. (Cognitive scientists see playing as developing.) At the heart of what it means to be a healthy human being we are all curious, playful, learners. This insight is often overlooked in the technology driven details that many golfers are attracted to when trying to make progress.

"Thinking too much over the ball can be a big problem. That's what I see in my amateur partners, who appear paralyzed from too much analysis. Some can't make even the easiest shot without running through a checklist." (Tiger Woods, *Golf Digest*, May 2008)

In playing-to-learn environments individuals playfully cooperate with problems to be solved, they do not challenge them. It's through playful cooperation with our environment that thinking and physical skills are unconsciously enhanced, as problems to be solved become partners for progress. Elements such as the wind, an uphill or downhill shot are elements that should be cooperated with, not challenged.

Some approaches to golf instruction have left out acts of playing-to-learn in favor of how-to directions from a perceived expert. The how-to directions do not enhance the deductive operations of spontaneous rapid reasoning that are connected to playful learning. "Concealed in the pure joy of playful participation is learning."[5] Interpretations can be wrong, but playful involvement is filled with real access to answers.

"Tiger Woods is appreciating the battle with boundless enthusiasm and passion, with a disposition that is closer to 'play' than that of nearly anyone else."[6] Being at play promotes learning through play.

In 1899, Karl Groos said, "human beings have a very long childhood so that we can play. We play for several years to pre-exercise the skills we need in the future." Groos organized his ideas of developing intelligence around the idea that we all play-to-learn. Groos believed back then what cognitive scientists believe today, that acts of play had to have a clear purpose (enhance intelligence); otherwise the natural biology of life would not have permitted the evolution of playful acts. Sigmund Freud said there was a clear developmental line that went from play to work. Unfortunately, the genius of play is often overlooked and undervalued.

Acts of play are not either cognitive, social, or emotional. During true play all three are combined.[7] In playing-to-learn environments the steps and stages of training and developing potentially become the end. It is by improving learning potential first that performance potential improves. That's why it is great to Play!

When it comes to thinking about the genius of play we could say there are two minds. One that is not aware of the true developmental value of playing-to-learn, and one that is very grateful. Because of the value of what science refers to as *indirect preparation*, every past twist and turn in an individual's life can help improve their golf skills (learning in one domain indirectly supports learning in other domains). It has been said that when learning anything, even golf, there is always less progress on a clear or linear path than on a path that presents a variety of problems to solve.

---

5 Jack Petrash, *Understanding Waldorf Education, Learning From the Inside Out*, pg 49

6 Brad Kearns, *How Tiger Does It*, pg 93

7 *The Development of Play*, pg 8

One Side of the Story

Perhaps, for years many golfers have only been made aware of one side of the story, and expect: (1) to be told what is wrong with their swing (2) told to copy an expert model (3) been given drills (4) had their swing compared to a tour professional on video replay (5) or been given how-to directions by a perceived expert. None of these five commonly used approaches to golf instruction are brain compatible for long-term learning. For example, respected research has shown that fixing isn't learning, but playing and experimenting normally is. Expert models are more valuable when used as inspirations rather than as models to copy. If used at all, video replay during instruction is not as useful as showing video ***after*** instruction, with the student doing the self-evaluation. Drills are more valuable after a skill is learned than they are for learning a skill. Following directions does not fully engage the higher cortex of the brain, where learning takes place. Unfortunately, the language of traditional approaches to progress promotes fixing, and not self-discovery learning.

The concept that the genius of play expands intelligence is being recognized by parents, coaches, educators, and employers who are sharing general non-specific ideas and suggestions rather than acting as evaluators of right and wrong. In playing-to-learn environments advice givers take on the roll of a facilitator of learning potential.

A master of anything was first a master of playing-to-learn! Play with the idea that any school, coach, parent, or employer who is trying to change poor outcomes without first enhancing learning potential, will not be as efficient as they could be. After a student's learning potential is enhanced their performance potential can improve.

In playing-to-learn environments there is no failure, only usable feedback for future use. Modern cognitive science and my own experience have found that a playing-to-learn approach to progress clearly gives a greater return on investment of time and resources than a learning-to-play (i.e., teaching-fixing to get-it-right) approach. The results are attention grabbing! Individuals not only learn faster, they retain skills and information longer in play-to-learn environments that are giving students choices and the opportunity to self-discover and self-evaluate. A choice, it has been said, is the most powerful thing an individual can be given when learning, as decision making, and self-evaluating are occurring. Following how-to directions is the least useful. Remember, we are human beings not human followers! There is nothing complicated about brain compatible learning principals - counter-intuitive - yes, but complicated - no. Playing-to-learn allows you to be yourself.

To be born, or "come into being," is the original Greek meaning of **ginesthi**, from which the common Latin word ***genius*** is derived. It is by living and ***being playful*** that our genius is revealed. While playing-to-learn environments may seem counter-intuitive, learning to play approaches are normally counterproductive. "When success is defined very narrowly (get it right), many individuals go through life feeling like a failure." Dr. Kenneth Ginsburg (*New York Times*, April 29, 2008)

A basic law of human development is that people are normally nervous about change. On the other hand people are normally not nervous about playing, which supports learning and reaching our optimal potential. Anything that is not brain compatible for learning should be rethought and redirected.

Self-Organizing Games

In a *New York Times* article by Bill Pennington, ("The Picture of Fair Play," January 3, 2004), Peter Roby, Director of Northeastern University Center for the Study of Sports and Society was quoted, *"There is a trend in athletics, one that continued to gain steam in 2003, one that has more and more children "deserting" traditional sports. Young people are now being drawn to the so called extreme sports of skate-boarding, in line skating, BMX biking, snowboarding and the X Games."* Roby went on to say, *"The organized pressures of other sports, and time spent away from overzealous adults (coaches and parents), is why kids are drawn to these environments."* Does anyone reading this believe that the skills used and performed at the X Games were not playfully self-organized and self-developed in a playful *learning-developing* environment? This is in contrast to a teaching-fixing to get-it-right approach to learning with a perceived expert (parents and coaches) offering how-to directions and technical details.

Adult learners also respond more favorably in a learning-developing environment free of how-to directions and the kind of stress they create.

The roots of reaching one's optimum potential are found in playful, supportive, non-judgmental environments. A knack for learning can be enhanced when fear, apprehension, and confusion are defused.

Individuals who are trying to make progress often have a heightened curiosity; some to the point that an "any port in a storm" approach takes over, as they consciously go from one theory to the next. Because human beings are wired to always look for what is novel (a survival skill), new and different information can be intellectually interesting, but at the same time educationally vacant.

Our brain is a malleable living organ, (not just a notebook to record information in) that can intuitively assemble proper connections, and this insight is often overlooked. Efficient approaches to learning draw individuals into acts of playful curiosity about their own questions. Efficient approaches to learning do NOT ask us to merely follow directions.

Why play-to-learn? Research from modern science has demonstrated that acts of play clearly grow new connections in our brain, develop intelligence, and promote learning. Environments that support play have no criticisms or corrections from a perceived expert that can lower self-confidence and slow down the pace of progress. **It could be argued that technical instruction created the need for mental coaches who are telling individuals to "free up your mind and just play."** Progressive development is about communication, not control. Pointing out what is wrong is the wrong approach to progress. According to Holley Silvers, Director of Research at the Santa Monica Orthopedic and Sports Medicine Research Foundation, "Once something is learned neurally, it is never unlearned. It never leaves you." Learning what to do is brain compatible; trying to change a habit is not.

The Conscious Mind, "I Don't Know How."

On July 6, 2008, an interviewer asked Tiger Woods (the world's number one golfer), "While having a serious injury and hardly any practice, how did you manage to win the U.S. Open at Torrey Pines a few weeks ago?" He answered, "I don't know."

On the same day (July 6, 2008), at the Wimbledon Tennis Tournament in the men's singles championship match (considered by some to be the greatest tennis match in the history of the game) Rafael Nadal beat the number one player in the world, Roger Federer, to win the championship. When asked how he did it, Nadal answered the same as Tiger, "I don't know." When Nadal was then asked what he was thinking about during the match, he replied "You don't think, if you think you can't play tennis." It is my guess that Tiger Woods would say the same about playing golf: that you cannot consciously think and play up to your potential. After winning the 2008 WGC Bridgestone Invitational Vijay Singh said, "I didn't think about anything but swinging the club. That's a good way to play."

For me, these "I don't know" answers from two great performers were on the mark accurate. Play with the idea that Woods' and Nadal's conscious thinking minds were not involved when playing, but their unconscious or subconscious minds were.

Tiger and Nadal were saying that they could not give a conscious reason for their accomplishments. Both these performers' actions in the present were clearly grounded in past experiences encoded in their unconscious minds. Said another way, unconscious, intuitive, spontaneous, and improvisational interactions with the environment are supported by the indirect preparation that past experiences provided.

Everyday we all do many things unconsciously, which if consciously thought about we would perform below our potential. Tiger Woods and Rafael Nadal's mental and physical interactions with the ever changing environments that golf courses and tennis matches present are two examples of how past experiences unconsciously flow through our actions in the present, causing individuals to say, "I just did it and I don't know how."

Our conscious mind has no past experience, but our unconscious mind is encoded with past experiences that have the ability to support and guide what we are doing in the present. When the indirect preparation of past experiences is guiding our actions, we often say, "I don't know how I did that," but our subconscious does.

I would like to repeat and emphasize that my ability to interact and communicate with students and their ability to make progress improved dramatically after I became aware of the information and research you are reading. **People who are not making progress may need more playful learning skills, not more *how-to* directions from well meaning friends.**

We could say every golfer who is not happy with their progress in golf has **a golf swing waiting to be born**. When people are learning other sports, they normally receive fewer how-to directions than when they are learning golf. This may be one reason their progress can be slower with golf than other sports.

A playful approach means you are open to self-discovery and are not following someone else's directions. Playful progress is guided, not taught. With a playful or a Zen approach (i.e., self-discovery) the beginner and master see and understand together and every intention becomes no intention. There is spontaneous playful discovery for every situation (i.e., a world-class golfer trusts their feel for the shot, even if it is the first time they are faced with it). Acts of play are personal, like the feel for a putt or a swing. **Environments that are geared for helping individuals are not as valuable as environments that geared for helping people help themselves.** Playing-to-learn approaches to progress are helping individuals to help themselves uncover many unexpected outcomes.

Play Enhances Our Intelligence

In 1994, a group of fifty-two (52) respected scholars formulated a scientific consensus and defined intelligence. Their definition of intelligence is in part of the article "Mainstream Science On Intelligence" (published in the *Wall Street Journal*), is as follows: "the ability to reason, plan, solve problems, think abstractly, comprehend complex ideas, learn quickly, and learn from experience; the ability to 'catch on', make sense of things, and figure out what to do."[8]

Studies from modern science points out that acts of play clearly enhance our intelligence and capacity for learning anything (even golf) by enhancing every item in this definition of intelligence. Workable learning environments are efficient because the work done by students becomes the enabler.

In their book, *Spark*, authors John J. Ratey MD and Erik Hagerman state: "Exercise and movement make the brain function at its best. They cue the building blocks of learning in the brain." Readers should play with the idea that any attempt to learn and make progress that is not based on **brain-compatible learning principles will** be less valuable than it could be. The genius of play, developing, and learning are all one in the same. By exploring the brain, we explore insights into efficient learning.

The personal insights found in the genius of play seem to be the most useful mode of transportation for staying on a path to reach ones potential. Every child and every scientist is playing-to-learn. Golfers should be doing the same. **The genius of play gives information practical value that goes beyond being interesting to our intellect.**

Let's play around with another idea; playing-to-learn is the most rewarding approach to progress any individual (young or old) could choose. Everyone who is reading these words has played and fooled around with more than a few things while learning to use them, or while making progress with a skill. We have also watched others do the same, as the uncontrolled freedom of play opened pathways to long-term progress found in the kind of imagination that has no plan,

---

8 *The Brain*, pg 109

just playful thoughts and actions. Playing-to-learn can be thought provoking. A mathematician is being playful with numbers, a novelist is being playful with words, a composer is being playful with sounds, and an artist is being playful with forms and colors. Golfers should be playful with different alignments for their golf clubs' face, head, and shaft through impact, to learn different ball flights suitable for different conditions.

> **Warning!** Every motion or reaction we make in our daily lives, including the motions of swinging a golf club, can be measured down to the smallest detail and unfortunately used as a model to copy. This kind of information is a technical, detailed description of motions that have already happened, with questionable value of future use (especially for learning golf). According to the Science of Learning, expert models are best used as inspirations, not as models to copy. "Tiger, from a very young age, did not care about how other people played golf. Tiger was not interested in following in somebody else's footsteps. The only thing on his mind was the ball, his club and to put the ball in the hole" (Rudy Duran, Tiger's first coach). Tiger once told a golf clinic audience, "One of the things my parents have taught me is never listen to other people's expectations."[9]

---

9 Brad Kearns, *How Tiger Does It*, pg 154

CHAPTER THREE
A Series of Essays

Pleasure vs. Perfection

Playing golf always offers some challenges, but if the game is going to be inviting, learning and making progress should be a pleasurable challenge. ***Pleasurable Game for All***[10] is what I feel the PGA of America call letters could stand for. In this early part of the twenty first century (2008), and for a number of years, for every golfer who takes up the game, another one stops playing and leaves the game. National Golf Foundation and other's surveys tell us that golf has become a zero growth industry. During the last 20 years it seems that the golf industry was focusing on perfection. The perfect golf ball, the perfect set of golf clubs; the perfect golf swing; and I could go on. For many, this focus on perfection put aside the pleasure of playing a game. Trying for perfection can create the kind of frustrations that makes the game of golf less inviting for individuals, and is not growing the game for the golf industry. Whether you are shooting 80 or 120 you should be able to enjoy your experience!

Interest grows when an activity is seen as pleasurable with fun following interest. When a golfer's interest in learning and playing a game is high, the natural ups and downs of anyone's learning curve are met with "Hey, this is interesting, I am staying involved." Some in the golf industry are saying that golf is a hard game to learn and to play. Well this just isn't so, and I am not sure that saying it is a hard game encourages people to start playing golf. There are blind golfers, one arm golfers, golfers with one leg, golfers who have played the game for only a few years and golfers who play only a few times a year who can shoot scores in the high 70s and low 80s.

As was said, golf should be pleasurable for all and in playing-to-learn environments it is. The way some information delivery systems are asking individuals to learn and play golf has made progress at an acceptable pace more difficult than it should be. There is little pleasure to be found in learning-to-play, teaching-fixing to get-it-right environments filled with how-to directions, technical details, and corrections that cause a loss of self-confidence. **Promoting**

---

10 "**P**leasurable **G**ame for **A**ll" and "**P**leasurable **G**olf for **A**ll" are trademarks of Learning Golf, Inc.

perfection and getting-it-right separates progress from brain compatible principles of learning. On the other hand, playing to learn environments promote aspirations, not technical details and perfection. In playing-to-learn environments individuals could be seen as travelers and explorers on a journey of self-discovery and self-evaluation. In a teaching-fixing environment, individuals are only visitors. In playing-to-learn environments we are interacting in ways that always support learning, and not fixing poor habits.

"It's useful to know that at its core learning is a biological event. For example, without directions, or consciously trying, during the first three or four years of our lives learning of such vastness happens that it over shadows all future learning. To approach learning consciously is a biological impossibility."[11] It is self-evident that early learning happened (unconsciously) in playing-to-learn environments that were brain compatible for learning. Tiger Woods said, "I've learned to trust my subconscious. My instincts have never lied to me."[12]

Individuals can be aware of what world class cooking is and what championship skiing entails, without taking any pleasure away from their own (less than perfect) acts of cooking or skiing. Why? Because both of these activities have been promoted as pleasurable, regardless of skill level, and not as activities that lead you to believe you have to have perfected them in order to enjoy them. Unfortunately, golfers are normally not given the opportunity to experience a safe, judgment free environment when learning and playing golf. "Tiger was an awesome golfer - but he didn't know anything specific, he learned by experimenting on his own and watching his father," Rudy Duran (Tiger's first coach). Playing-to-learn environments avoid the distractions that detailed information, and how-to directions create. When we feel in control of our own outcomes we don't have the stress of trying to follow someone else's directions.

---

11 *Magical Child*, pg 143

12 Earl Woods, *Start Something*, pg 106

The following is a letter to the editor of the *New York Times* in 2008:

Dear Editor (Sports),

I have enjoyed all of Bill Pennington's "On Par" columns, especially "Shaving Strokes and Integrity" on July 14th, about golfers bending the rules when they play. Clinical psychologist Dr. Wayne Glad was quoted, "There is intense pressure on golfers to be good," as a cause. Reading that 70% of the 7000 golfers questioned, and 85% of the top 400 business executives said they have cheated when playing golf was eye opening.

Perhaps this pressure to break the rules that Dr. Glad mentioned is fueled when golf is promoted as a game of perfection, side stepping the pure pleasure of playing a game. The perfect swing, the perfect club, the perfect ball, is what golfers are always hearing, and some are making up their own perfect scores.

*The PGA of America could promote that there call letters, PGA to stand for **P**leasurable **G**ame for **A**ll. Perhaps this would move the mind set some golfers seem to have beyond just the score they shoot, into recognizing everything else playing golf offers.*

*The term "play" could stand for **P**owerful **L**earning **A**bout **Y**ourself. What golfers could learn about themselves by enjoying the companionship of others, physical exercise, and the green grass experience, would be different than what they experience when seeking perfection. Frustrations and pressure to bend the rules could be the result of a perfection versus pleasure environment. As Bill Pennington said, bending the rules cheats the player and a game that can be pleasurable for all when a golfer's mind-set moves beyond just seeking perfection.*

Michael Hebron

Learning and Playing Golf

This essay is based mostly on H. W. Rollins's insights into learning and playing golf. These are ideas for learning golf that I believe Rollins would say that the way to know their value is to apply them.

Rollins said, his ideas are "intended for contemplation, only fundamental principles are included, with any reality of understanding left for the reader to discover." Nothing is intended to replace or interfere with a player's active feel. Even when making a change in form, the player should swing the club with as much personal feel as possible. The most important part of any shot, is always its feel.

Many golf ideas deal with form, but the only purpose of the form is to enhance our feel through cooperation with natural laws. Form and feel are two sides of the same coin. Form is confining without feel, and feel is unreliable without form. There is a balance that the player has to find. **Fortunately, balance is found in a swing that unconsciously swings itself.**

Improving one's golf is not so much a matter of acquiring ability as it is a matter of becoming aware of an ability that already exists. Improving one's golf is a process of discovering pre-existing abilities and allowing them to come through unhindered. Any effort required is only to become comfortable with effortlessness, while still maintaining a sense of purposeful action.

When the game is broken down into components it should only be for the convenience of personal observations. In reality, the components are merely different personal reflections of one whole. It's through application of a swing that the components merge back into the whole, which is the only complete experience of playing golf.

Playing

Freedom

Play each shot as if you found yourself confronted with only that shot.

Decide what you want to do, then take hold of the club and swing trying to hit the ball where you want it to go. **Disregard the score.**

Believing

Know that if you do something once, you can do it again.

Believe that each shot you are about to play will be as good as your best ever.

Enjoyment

Always appreciate the opportunity to play golf.

Allow yourself the experience of complete enjoyment.

Love the game.

Learning

A Definition and Purpose of Learning

Learning is the process of awakening to new perspectives, and most of all new understanding, and new applications of what is already known.

The purpose of learning is to expand awareness.

The Requirements of the Player or Learnist: (Chemistry has chemists, education has learnists.)

- A learnist decides if their current awareness is unsatisfactory.
- A learnist defines what they want to learn.

- A learnist desires to learn with an attitude that says, "I will."
- A learnist takes responsibility for their own progress.
- A learnist views their mistakes as acceptable and necessary feedback.
- A learnist exercises the fullness of their patience.
- A learnist understands that they can only use the ability they believe they have.

The Process of Learning

The player or learnist seeks to understand cause and effect and seeks to master the cause that produces the desired effect.

The player or learnist tries their hand at the application of a new insight with the intention of becoming aware of a workable execution.

The player or learnist focuses on doing what is needed, rather than on what they want to fix. (Very important!)

The player or learnist accepts that learning is a process to which there is no end.

Training and Practice

Fundamentals of Effective Training

The purpose of training is to learn and develop the physical and mental skills required to play golf.

Define what you are training, such as acts of swinging the club.

Always have an objective in mind.

Take each shot as seriously as any other shot.

Break off and regain being engaged when concentration wavers.

Move on when the objective is accomplished.

Training Form

The purpose of training our form is to achieve or rediscover the feel of our swing.

Make practice swings when making changes.

Train only one thing at a time.

Practice simple short shots.

When workable outcomes arrive, begin practicing feel.

Practicing Feel

The purpose of training feel is to deepen and broaden the feel of a shot by applying it creatively to different circumstances. (Very important)

Simulate playing conditions as much as possible.

Practice variety rather than repetitions.

Practice simple, medium and difficult shots.

Practice having a picture and the feel before the shot.

Reversing the Flow

The tendency in the pursuit of form is to first learn from outside to in, using the outer form (see the whole swing) to create the inner awareness. This is as it should be. **But once you experience the full awareness of one motion and one feel, you have what the pursuit of form is intended to give you.** Then you must begin to learn from inside out, allowing the inner awareness to create the outer form - a swing that unconsciously swings itself.

To use this creative flow, the awareness of one motion and one feel become the intention, or cause. You know from experience that the awareness exists, so it is a matter of tuning into it, allowing yourself to experience it again. See and feel the stroke before you swing.

Then the concerns of form will begin to unconsciously take care of themselves. The extent to which you tune into that unconscious awareness (seeing and feeling) is the extent to which it will manifest in the shot.

To do this you must take a calm, firm, and unwavering stand within yourself. You must insist absolutely that you can and will perform at the height of your ability. **Whether or not you play up to your ability is inconsequential. Your previous experience of the feel is the foundation of your resolve.**

Application

Overview

Let's look at the task of playing actual shots. You are not just going out and hoping for the best, but you are using your current ability to unconsciously create the experience you want. When playing golf you have to use whatever awareness is available to you. This application is useful no matter what your current level of awareness is. **It is intended to allow you to use the current height of your ability, no matter what height that happens to be.** This is *being* a golfer, not becoming one. It does not matter if you do not have the full awareness of one motion and one feel yet (which is **the swing that unconsciously swings itself**). The purpose of *playing* is to relieve yourself from consciously thinking about the parts and allowing yourself to just play golf unconsciously.

When you have felt the effortless simplicity of a swing that unconsciously swings itself, even once, you'll know it. Knowing that is the experience of an ability that already exists. But it is not possible to get it once and then sit back and try to have it forever. You must always allow it; always expand your awareness of it by applying what you have learned. There is no limit to the intensity and consistency of that awareness.

Although this application can be divided into components, no distinct lines should be drawn between them. The more you understand one the more it becomes the whole. **The thought**

becomes the feeling and the feeling becomes the unconscious action. It is a continuum where one thing flows seamlessly into the next and then back into the others. Understanding and trusting it brings on the complete experience of playing golf with **a swing that unconsciously swings itself**.

The Present Moment (Thought)

Playing golf is the cumulative art of unconsciously swinging the club and hitting shots. However, only one shot can be played at a time. It is not possible to replay the last shot, nor is it possible to skip ahead and play the next one. Therefore, stay engaged with the now and play the shot that confronts you. You are only capable of acting in the present, so be in the present so that your past experiences can help you act effectively. There is no past or future with a swing that unconsciously swings itself. This is *being* a golfer, not becoming one.

You accomplish this by observing and being engaged with the requirements of the shot that confronts you. The most useful swing model for anyone is the requirements of the shot about to be played. See what the course is asking for. See what the possibilities are for the shot by taking in all the information necessary to make an unconscious but informed decision about what shot to play. **Choose the swing that best accommodates the combination of influences for the pending shot (observing the course conditions and all other considerations that you are aware of). The course is speaking to you!**

Intention (Feeling)

We should pre-create the shot based on our decision from our observations mentioned above. See the shot in the mind's eye before you play it. Intend it to be workable. Begin to create some feeling and image of it in your mind. See the ball going where you want it to go. Feel the shot you want to play, the set-up, the swing, impact, the finish, everything as a whole not as parts. See it and feel it as intensely as possible. All of this becomes one awareness of that shot.

Approach the ball with one awareness and enter unconsciously into your set-up. The feel you have created contains the set-up, so it is just a matter of following the feel with the body. The position is there, and all you have to do is keep awareness and simply melt into it without using words. When the set-up is workable, it intensifies the awareness even further. Tiger Woods' first coach, Rudy Duran, would say, "You already know, now to do it."

Execution (Action)

When the set-up is complete with the awareness intact, there's nothing consciously left to do but swing. The feel in the set-up contains the swing, so again it is a matter of following the feel with the body. **The swing is already there** and all you have to do is keep awareness - see it, feel it - and let it unconsciously swing itself. It may seem effortless. All you have to do is take hold of the club, swing and try to hit the ball where you want it to go. Just hit it knowingly!

While what you have just read may seem counter-intuitive, it is a brain compatible approach to learning and playing golf. In 2008, Tiger Woods said, "I do not know how I did that" after making a 20-foot putt to win Arnold Palmer's tournament on the last hole at Bay Hill. Because of what he had learned from past experiences, he unconsciously made that putting swing. His memory made that putt and any conscious attempt would not have produced the same outcome.

The No-Swing Golf Swing

The title of a small booklet (14 pages) is *Stewart MacDougall's Complete Instruction Book, Golf — The No Swing Golf Swing.* The inside cover reads, "This book is an instruction guide for learning golf." What follows are some of MacDougall's suggestions and insights about learning golf.

This Scottish professional opens by saying, "Reams of advice have been written about the game and how to play it. This booklet shows you how to start the learning process.

"If you have most of your extremities you can play golf. If you can stand up you can play golf. If you can drive a nail with a hammer you can play golf. If you can dance, you can play very good golf, so let's dance.

"Golf clubs and hammers are close relatives. There are tools for every job and clubs for every shot.

"A golf swing is like a finger print: no two are alike. Your swing is your swing and as you adapt and make small changes, you will also improve your rhythm, but your swing is yours.

"The most important idea about the golf swing is that it's a movement performed with very little physical effort.

"In the learning you will be offered a lot of advice about how to swing the golf club. These platitudes are personal perceptions of what may work and they can be dangerous to your health. What is really being said is that your swings don't look right, and nine out of ten times you have forgotten our first rule - relax, stand up, which are the basics for the no-swing-golf swing (i.e., a non-conscious golf swing).

"The most underrated move in the golf swing is the start. It's the foundation of the 'no-swing golf swing.' If you get this, you will be able to play golf well forever.

"This is a natural swinging movement: a smooth release of power created by letting your golf club do the driving.

"This creates power (force) without really trying. With some practice you will experience power without physical effort.

"Our brain is our personal computer and it will find distance and direction for the shot.

"Golf's fundamentals sooner or later will produce good results. Practice helps lady luck to smile on you!

"Is that all there is? No - there is a life time of experimenting, trying this and that, looking for what works for you. The wonderful thing about golf, it's never over, you never conquer."

I would suggest that you see yourself as training, and after something is learned then see yourself as practicing it. When spending time on your golf game with a mind-set that feels like practicing before something is learned normally creates frustration. Train, then practice.

A 10% Theory

When it comes to making long term progress, unfortunately learning-to-play approaches to progress often have golfers spending 90% of their training time on just 10% of what can make a golfer good, or even great. Try making your own list of all the elements you believe can make a golfer good. What makes Tiger Woods, Annika Sorenstam, and Lorena Ochoa great golfers? What made Jack Nicklaus, Lee Trevino, and Ben Hogan great?

If the list of elements that makes golfers good is accurate, it will not be a short list. We could start a list with their swing, and then add imagination, emotional control, ability to focus, physical strength, flexibility, short game skills, reasoning powers, deduction skills, eyesight, organization skills, memory, self-discipline, past experience, self-confidence, training schedule, and I could go on. Note that the golf swing was only one of the elements on the list of what can make a golfer good or great (and not the most important). Unfortunately, many golfers are spending 90% of their time with less than 10% of what can make a golfer good; their golf swing. After Padridge Harrington won the 2008 PGA Championship he said, "A fantastic win, but I did not have my swing this week."

When a golfer swings and the results is an unwanted outcome (below their current potential), it has less to do with their physical ability to swing the club, and more to do with how efficient all the other elements on our list allow the swing to happen. This holds true for high and low handicap golfers as well as professionals. We all know golfers with less than classic golf swings who play good golf, and professionals who win when they do not have their "A" game. "Tiger didn't think about his swing. His sole mission was to hit the ball at the target" said Tiger's first coach, Rudy Duran. This is an example of true engagement with learning.

Playing-to-learn approaches to progress are similar to being a general manager who is taking a wide focus to enhance every element that could support reaching optimum potential. On the other hand, learning-to-play approaches have much narrower focus, such as focusing only on the golf swing. For example, a learning-to-play approach in golf might be one that uses technical details about the golf swing, how-to directions to fix the golf swing, or expert models to copy a golf swing. Golf is not a game called "golf swing," it's a game of playing golf.

When playing golf for perfection, or trying for a certain score, it's unlikely that you will ever be happy on the course.

Being a competent golfer doesn't require mastering a lot of technical knowledge or developing a perfect swing. "You have to care, but you can't care about the results." (Loren Roberts) The fifteenth club in our bag is the "forget-it" club. Tom Lehman, winner of 19 tournaments on the PGA Tour, and the 1996 British Open said "I came out of a long putting slump because of the simple insight that the brain can't process two thoughts at the same time. I'd had all this stuff consciously in mind about the break, speed, and the stroke. Now my mantra is "roll it into the middle of the hole." (*Golf Digest*, May 2008)

Indirect Preparation

"One of the most important discoveries from learning science research is that learning *always* takes place against a backdrop of existing knowledge."[13] (Past experiences are a form of indirect preparation for new learning.) The term a "transfer of learning" makes reference to how past experiences flow through new learning, allowing new information to be transferred more efficiently to long term memory. When we are encoding new information, depending on one's past experiences, it's either useful or not - but it is always meaningful. **Past experiences reveal our options, not the answer.**

Golf is a game, and like all games we play there are some obvious benefits including; spending time outdoors, having fun, exercising the body in a leisure time activity while enjoying the company of others. Golf is a game of solving problems by asking ourselves question about the ever-changing environments a golf course presents. There are also some counter-intuitive benefits from learning and playing golf. More than other sports, golf seems to engage mankind's higher cortex.

A less obvious benefit of learning and playing golf is that every mental skill a golfer engages during these acts can be transferred to other learning opportunities in school, businesses, different sports and other walk of life. Mankind is a creative problem solving being that is learning all the time through the *indirect preparation* and *parallel processing* founded on our past experiences. New experiences "flow through" and mix with all of our past experiences birthing new learning that then develops into new knowledge, or the know-how of using information.

The physical and mental skills used when learning and playing golf are a form of indirect preparation that can unconsciously flow into other learning environments. These skills include reasoning, decision making, self-control, self-discovery, body motions, self-assessment, self-development, and self-learning to name a few. Acts of learning and playing golf are supported by past experiences from our every day interactions. All segments of our life produce personal insights about

13 *The Learning Sciences*, pg 11

balance, timing, problem solving, etc., that are indirect preparation for learning and playing golf. Golf is a game, within the larger game of life's experiences

Acts of learning, like everything else that influences in mankind's body and brain are a biological process that is grounded in an individual's past experiences. While this may be a counter intuitive insight, it's an accurate one. Studies show both similar and dissimilar past experiences make up the *indirect preparation* for what we are doing and learning in the present.

When individuals are going through the trial and feedback (never failure) of becoming familiar with the design of a golf club and optimum approaches for using it, many valuable lessons are being encoded that can be used beyond golf environments. Biologically, (all learning is biological in nature) it is not possible to learn directly just from our experiences in the now. Interactions in the present are being simultaneously cross-referenced with past experiences (indirect preparation) that guide efficient acts of learning in the now with golf and beyond.

The stage of learning that is called parallel possessing is: what is going on in the now is paralleled to and cross-referenced with the patterns, sequences, perceptions, and classifications that are formed from what we have already experienced.

Again, when performing or learning a particular activity or taking in new information, these acts are guided by the indirect preparation (or past experiences) encoded in our subconscious.

Learning to play golf goes way beyond developing your golf swing (which is less than 10% of the game). Learning to play golf is about learning the skills of seeing options; making your own choices, using your own reasoning and deduction skill. It is also about taking risks, self-control, persistence, being creative, using imagination, learning to self-discover, self-evaluation, and emotional stability. These and other skills, that are enhanced when playing to learn golf, are indirectly transferred to other learning environments including schools, businesses, other sports, etc. Golf is indeed a thinking man's game that can stimulate minds in the direction of sense making higher order thinking.

Some deeply significant research has shown that individuals from all age groups (child to adult) can indirectly enhance their ability to learn while they are in school, attending seminars, doing workshops, or in any other organized learning environment, through what they experience and interact with beyond formal education settings. In other words, what you learn in one setting can greatly help you in other settings.

The kind of intelligence and higher order thinking that is at the heart of the nature of learning is the same kind of intelligence used when playing games, especially when playing golf. Respected instructor Chuck Hogan said, "it's unfortunate that the intelligence of play is often overlooked and undervalued." Efficient approaches for learning anything join the nature of play and learning skills with core subject matter information.

Playing sports, golf in particular, can be the kind of indirect preparation that has a positive educational influence on enhancing learning potential. The constructive nature and activities that are at the core of playing golf produce the kind of mind-brain development that enhances self-learning skills. Of all games, golf seems to have the most value added components (self skills) when it comes to supporting and enhancing one's ability to learn through self-discovery. To quote respected instructor Susan Berdoy Meyers "Golfers learn to initiate and create movements on their own through self-discovery."

Golf has always been more of a thinking man's game than a physical sport. It's a game played by individuals who are making decisions without the support of teammates, or a coach who is calling set plays. Golf is played under conditions that are always changing. Every golf course and every golf hole is unique - no two are the same. In playing-to-learn environments golfers learn to make their own choices, see their options, and use their own reasoning and deduction skills before every swing. In playing-to-learn environments golfers develop flexible knowledge and portable skills.

Each time a golfer swings their golf club they are challenged by the peculiar and unique circumstances the golf course and environment present at the moment of the particular swing. Before a golfer swings they have attempted to evaluate and make sense of the shot they are about to play. After this evaluation takes place, a golfer now goes through their options for creating successful outcomes, deciding which of their 14 clubs they will use. As golfers become more experienced they also make a choice of what type of ball flight they want to create (high-low, left to right, right to left, straight, etc.).

Ideally golfers have learned to be prepared. Hopefully, they are prepared to be spontaneous, improvisational, and creative (not consistent) with the following.

Reasoning powers	**Conquering inhibitions**
Deduction skills	Focusing
Self-control	Restraint of impulses
Memory	Cooperation
Observation abilities	Discouragement
Social Development	Endurance
Respect for Rules	Development of will
Work ethic	Emotional stability
Risk taking	Imagination
Goal setting	Creativity
Determination	Anticipation
Self-development	Self-evaluation
Self-discovery	Decision-making
Predicting	Summarizing
Clarifying	Questioning
Seeing patterns	Seeing connections

Creativity vs. Details

Becoming educated is less about knowing the details of a particular skill or fact, than about being able to find your own way of creating workable outcomes by using basic core information. While he was injured, Tiger Woods won the 2008 US Open by adjusting and creating workable, not perfect outcomes with the same playful skills and imagination he came to golf with as a young child. As John Paul Newport wrote in the *Wall Street Journal* (6/21/2008), "Tiger put concerns aside so that he could become absorbed in executing a pure, intuitive swing." **It seems that traditional approaches to golf instruction are grounded in a culture of teaching a swing, and not learning a variety of ways to use a golf club.** What set of problems will a "teach-a-swing" approach equip golfers to solve? What set of problems will learning a variety of ways to use a golf club equip golfers to solve? Playing to learn environments equip golfers to be creative with their golf club.

In the book *Games*, by Jessie H. Bancroft, published in 1909, he points out, *"Games have a positive educational influence that no one can appreciate who has not observed their effects. The use of play for both children and adults has deep significance for the individual's physical, mental and moral vitality. By playing, those who are observing little of what goes on around them; who react slowly to external stimuli; who are slow to see, think, or to do, can be completely transformed. The courage to take risks, to act impulsively, choosing between several different possible modes of play with individual initiatives, comes through playing. The rewards of play are all based upon a natural evolution of physical and psychological powers. Anyone charged with the education or training of students should know the results of modern studies in these particulars. We have come to realize that play is nature's own way of developing and training."* (Note these insights were written in 1909.)

Nature has always known what the science of learning has recently been uncovering, that **mankind plays to learn**. Again, human beings are born playful, playing to learn, not learning to play. Studies show that the *higher cortex* of our brain is opened and expanded through play, thereby improving our thinking, reasoning, creativity, and learning skills. Play and movement are both essential to long-term memory. A number of misconceptions about play and movement have caused them to be seen as less than noble acts, but current research shows that play and movement expand man's capacity to learn. The classic best sellers *Magical Child*, by Joseph Chilton Pearce, and *Absorbent Mind*, by Maria Montessori, also document how important acts of play are to encoding long-term learning.

There is an art or Zen like quality to playing good golf. For a moment let's add the words Art and Zen to the title of this book - which would now be The Art and Zen of Playing Golf to Learn Golf. The words *Art*, *Zen*, *Playing*, *To*, *Learn*, and *Golf* are defined in *Webster's Dictionary* as follows:

Art: The free use of imagination; a creative skill used.

Zen: Enlightenment achieved though innovation and simplicity.

Playing: Unconstrained movements; to give free play to one's imagination

To: In the direction of; for the purpose of.

Learn: To experience; to acquire.

Golf: A game played outdoors with a small ball and sticks.

The insights found in these six definitions should be kept in mind as one reads on about learning and improving golf. By using these definitions, the suggestion to golfers here is: the goal is the free use of playful imagination which is a creative skill, used to achieve enlightenment through intuition and simplicity, with the full play of one's imagination, for the purpose of moving in the direction of experiencing a game called golf, played outdoors with a small ball and sticks. Imagination is more powerful than a listing of details when it comes to long-term learning.

Movement

It may be useful to have some insights into why our bodies move. Every human has an internal system that is responsible for movement. The brain, spinal cord, cells, and other fibers make up what is known as our nervous system. It is within this system that firing neurons cause an exchange of chemical information in the spinal cord that is then sent on to the motor cortex of the brain to be interpreted. This information is then communicated to the appropriate muscle group to create the desired movements.

Information must be decoded then communicated efficiently by our brain before appropriate movements will occur in our bodies. The key words are *decoded* and *communicated*; progress with motor skills is always based on interpretation and communication. **When we trust using the information our nervous system naturally gathers, progress with our game is accelerated.**

Faults can arise when the brain's natural and reliable system of gathering, decoding, and communicating information is interrupted by conscious reinterpretation brought on by our fears, doubts, and self-talk, such as, "I never par this hole." Studies have shown that using words instead of visualizations often prevents students from reaching their potential. "Words can communicate only between those who share similar experiences." (Alan Watts) ***A picture is worth a thousand words only when words are not used to describe it!***

Start with a Mental Picture

When individuals begin to overuse words or consciously think too carefully about actions, the mind will not be creative or make timely decisions. The golfer whose mind is filled with words and thoughts does not react to or trust what he sees, hears, and feels. The natural system of learning from playful action can be paralyzed by thoughts and words. The suggestion here is to *see it and feel it* before you swing.

Golfers who are just trying to perform mechanical motions are not learning to play golf. This is similar to students who are taking in information to give back on a test without gaining any personal meaning for using the information beyond the classroom.

The Laws of Motion tell us that once you have created a force and you influence the direction of that force you can influence the direction of what the force hits. To take full advantage of this law, a sound golf stroke swings the weight of the club on a path that has a relationship to a target. Because of this swing assignment, the golfer should develop a swing that uses efficient energy without any unnecessary compensatory movements. **The swing has a beginning and an ending, with nothing but swinging in the middle, is a useful visualization.**

How we swing the club is determined by our mind-set, which is determined by how we are learning golf; through the genius of play versus with technical information.

One of the steps in making progress in golf or any other physical activity is understanding that, "the brain, while it does not swing the club, can stop the swing." (Dave Pelz) Golf is mental, physical and emotional. The body normally does what the brain commands. Everything the human body does starts in the brain first.

Our brain can be thought of as a "split brain" with two different hemispheres. The left side stores and uses verbal information, while the right side stores and uses visual information. Play with the idea that eyes do not see, ears do not hear, hands do not feel, and the nose does not smell; they all bring information to the brain to accomplish these interactions with the environment.

Efficient learning requires a brain compatible approach to progress, or teaching with the brain in mind. The body moves for one of these reasons: reflexes, anticipation, and when the right side of the brain gives the body a picture to copy. My suggestion to golfers is **to playfully learn golf with more of the right side of the brain than the left**. Pictures, feelings, and general non-specific concepts can be more useful than words when learning any motor skill (golf included). Consider when the Olympic diver is about to perform, or the tennis star is about to serve, or the fisherman is about to cast his line. They all have a *clear picture or feel* of what they are about to do before the body goes into action. I doubt their minds are filled with any technical details.

Play with the idea that all golf shots use brain work followed by club path, face angle and ball flight. The brain controls the body, the body controls the club, and the club controls the ball. **When the club is swinging efficiently (for the shot about to be played) the body will also be moving efficiently.** We did not learn how to move our body parts; we learned *what-to-do* with things (i.e., how to use a knife, toothbrush, button, etc.). The golfer's task is to learn what-to-do with the golf club under the variety of circumstances presented to them on the golf course. Focusing on how to move one's body is not as useful as learning what to do with the golf club for the shot at hand.

When the club face impacts the ball, they are joined and stay together for about one seventeen-thousandths of a second and three quarters of an inch before the ball separates from the club face. During this contact time and space the ball is being programmed by the swinging club. We could say the ball is being told to either go up, down, left, right, long, short. See the ball as a computer, the swing as the program, and the ball flight as the printout caused by what you did with the golf club.

Based on what you want to do with the golf club, our brain provides a very reliable and accurate system of telling our body what to do. **Our brain created the swing we produced (not our body)**; it did not happen by chance. The process started in the brain, moved to the body, then to the club and finally to the ball. If the brain can accurately tell the body and club what to do, why is it that many golfers do not play up to their potential?

First, at times the golfer's perception of the swing may be filled with too many details or false information. Next, self-interference; at times the golfer over thinks and does not playfully react. When learning or improving a motor skill, we should use the language and vocabulary of the brain, especially for the right side of the brain. Again, the language of the right side of the brain is pictures, feelings, and general non-specific concepts, not words. **Picturing what to do with the club, not how to move the body, is the suggestion here.**

Studies show communication is said to be only 5% words; that 85% of the information your brain receives and stores has come from the eyes, and 50% of what we hear is forgotten immediately. The best way a golfer's mind can communicate with his body is to picture and feel the shot beforehand (no words). Recalling the feel of the last successful shot, even if it was a chip or putt, is going to help. It is important to understand that playing golf is a creative process. Your ability to create will be influenced by the information your brain receives from past experiences and your eyes and how you then react and use this information.

It will be much easier for most of us to create a sound swing from a personal visual suggestion than from how-to directions. Students who prefer detailed written directions are called left-brain learners. While their preference may be for words and detail, the suggestion from learning science is to find visual keys (right-brain information) to improve a motor skill like golf. (Again, picture what to do with the club, not *how-to* move the body.)

Efficient approaches to progress use information that students already possess and direct the innate ability to playfully learn that every student brings with them to their golf experience. Students improve when they define and recall what is needed through acts of play, in contrast to what they have done in the past, or are currently doing. The human brain is very efficient. When you drop a glass of water you have done everything correctly to drop the glass. When you top the ball, you have done everything perfectly to top the ball. *You have not moved incorrectly.*

You may not like the outcome of your actions, but please recognize your actions started in the brain first. It is your own personal perception of the motor skill that is going to create pictures and feel for your brain. Motor skill actions are mostly unconscious imitations of the sum total of all the information the brain has of this skill at the time. Even new students have some preconception of performing a golf stroke. How the student perceives the skill is the first step in performing a motor skill. **Just-in-the-ball-park concepts are much more useful than technical details.**

Learning to improve a motor skill can become more successful when thought of as playful modifying behavior rather than correcting errors, or trying to exchange an unnecessary habit for a new or better one. Most of the time motor skills are helped by subtracting information not by adding to it. Studies show we can improve by taking technical details away and simplifying our perception of the swing.

Since the means of learning a motor skill can come from the various senses that perceive the activity, how and to what degree a student may learn the activity is based on the approach (delivery system) used to present information. Studies show that telling the body how to do something with words is not the most effective way to improve performance. **Our muscles don't understand words, and the thinking mind does not understand eye hand coordination.** Instructional information should not try to teach the swing, but it should help students redefine their insights and their personal perception of the swing, letting learning be random acts of self-discovery.

Research confirms that most of us learn more in our first five years than in all the rest of our lives. Yet as children we don't go through the process of trying to do it right; we don't try to learn, we simply do it. Adults can retard the learning process by their attachment to conceptualization or left-brain information (words and technical details).

My own preference has always been for random right-brain learning. Learning a motor skill requires awareness of what you see and feel in order to recall visualizations and feelings. Let's play with the idea of renaming critical thinking, problem solving, and imagination as *"unconsciously becoming aware of options."*

Following *how-to* directions can suppress awareness! I am suggesting that we should not use words to tell our body what to do. Avoid *how-to* instruction, which is an order from the mind of one person (instructor) to the body of another (student). The problem lies in our inability to translate verbal commands into body action; again muscles do not understand words. Using words that invoke an abstract description of movement will not help. It is an *image-rich language of familiar pictures* that should be used. **Past feelings from other actions or different skills can be very important and useful when learning any new motor skill.**

We must be encouraged to trust in our own capacity to learn from our own experiences and to have faith in what we see, hear, and feel. The role of instruction is to help students interpret the most relevant parts of experiences. Nature designed mankind to learn by *doing*, *observing* outcomes, and then *adjusting* as we see fit, based on the indirect preparation of our past experiences.

Experience and awareness simply sees and accepts what is and does not place a positive or negative value on results. Al Geiberger, PGA Champion, who once shot 59 in competition said, "I've come to realize I perform best when my subconscious mind plays the shot." When playing badly, your mind is filled with self-instruction, self-judgment, doubt, and fear of failure. When playing well your mind is relaxed, absorbed in the present, quiet, and free of tension. Athletes often call this experience "playing out of one's mind," a state free of mental interference frequently called "playing in the zones." **Being out of our thinking-mind when playing golf is the aim.**

It could be argued that technical information filled with details created the need for mental coaches who are suggesting - just play, don't think!

Being vs. Becoming

Being vs. Becoming was influenced by insights I gained from Clark McKowan's book, *Teaching Human Beings,* and *Teaching as Learning*, a book by Clark Moustakas.

It seems that the most useful entry point for making progress is through *being* who we are. When a low, or medium, or highly skilled performer has an open connection with their current skill level, (without judgment of outcomes), suddenly a light goes on and valuable insights arrive. By embracing *being* who we are, and our current skill level, the *self* in self-discovery and self-assessment is upgraded, supporting one's pace of progress.

BEING	BECOMING
Being is growth motivation	Becoming is deficiency motivated
Being involves inventing and choosing	Becoming often means following a prescribed path to make up for deficits.

Being is personal and unique; a positive self-fulfilling force.

Being is acting in terms of positive growth, not in terms of an absence.

Being is a form of incubation, becoming is not.

Being is tailored to fit and inhabit what motivates each unique individual with the common purpose of growing in the direction of enhancing learning potential.

Play with the idea that focusing is an act of seeking, while embracing is an act of letting-in. Focusing on becoming better with the details of the golf swing does not enhance the tools of advancement found in *being* one's self, while accepting and embracing outcomes without judgment. Acts of becoming and detailed information about the golf swing often create blind spots that fragment progress. When trying to become there is little authentic learning. Should golfers see themselves as *being* a golfer, or becoming a better golfer?

Trying to become a better golfer (or anything) and *being* a golfer (or anything) are not the same. It's by *being* a golfer at every level, (from new to experienced and not judging outcomes), that developmental learning takes hold and optimum potential can be experienced. The experience of *being* opens acts of growing, namely the experience of *being* who we are at the moment. By embracing all outcomes (workable and unworkable) that we have created as feedback for future reference, and we are *being* a golfer who is making progress. What works and what does not are equally meaningful to the nature of being one with the learning process. **"Outcomes are to be observed rather than explained, described, or categorized. John Dewey pointed out what is not explicitly present makes up a vastly greater part of an experience than does the conscious to which thinkers have so devoted themselves. Significant experiences should be pointed to, rather than explained."** (Clark E. Moustakas[14]) Detailed information often leaves individuals anxious and disoriented.

The most human form of learning demands a greater say from the receivers of information than following details normally provides. "Without the personal self in the experience there can be no real growth. It is we who emerge in experiencing something, and what we emerge into is the truth about that thing." (John Dewey[15])

Being and freedom are synonymous. John Dewey said, "freedom has three elements:

(1) efficiency in action and the absence of groping,

(2) capacity to change, to experience novelties,

(3) the power of desire and choice to be factors in events"[16]

The process of *being* is increasingly self-educated through freedom. There is fullness in freedom and variety. As a free *being*, poor outcomes are only temporary detours along the way to personal growth, continuing on in forms of new development and creation.

---

14 Clark Moustakas, *Teaching as Learning*, pg 12

15 Clark Moustakas, *Teaching as Learning*, pg 11, quoting Dewey

16 *Teaching as Learning*

To be positively free is being simultaneously spontaneous, thoughtful, self-enhancing, accepting and responsible. There is no freedom without responsibility. Self-assessment and self-confirmation are early forms of responsibility. Using our own senses to confirm or deny the quality of outcomes is the act of *being* in charge of one's own self. To accept the happenings and consequence of our actions and then move on is the process of *being* a lifelong learner. Again, when trying to become there is little authentic learning. It is by *being* that learning arrives.

Clark Moustakas wrote, "The real world of the learner is a world of personal meaning and involvement, a world centered in the *self*, with individual and peculiar forms of interests, activities, and concerns. Although it is important to meet the learner intellectually and cognitively, it is much more important to keep values in the forefront in learning. In no way should human values be neglected - sensitivity, awareness, uniqueness, freedom, responsiveness, respect for the integrity of the learner and his preferences and interests, authenticity, honesty, truth, love. Each of these human values has its place in everyday meetings and each is more important than the most important fact or skill. In no way should expediency, efficiency, organization and achievement push the *self* of the learner away, for the *self* of the learner is his one unique contribution to humanity. To let this inner light be dimmed is to destroy the potentials and powers of the *self*, which alone can create the lust for learning that carries the person beyond the region of the dull and commonplace into the ingenious and the creative, beyond the narrow confines of intellect and into the world of the senses, beyond security and status and into the responsiveness of communal living and lonely solitude, with all the pain and all the joy of human existence."

Golf Thoughts

Be aware of what's actually happening.

Progress comes from more awareness, and more feel.

As you playfully make changes, become comfortable with feeling uncomfortable.

The most valuable instructors and coaches help the learner become more aware and more self-confident.

Efficient motor skill instructors help change the way learners see things, they do not try to change what they do.

Efficient instructors and learners are more interested in the experience, than the explanation of motion.

People often can explain a motion - but will not see progress until they can experience it.

Do not try and fix - playfully let things happen until the feel is different.

Learning is building self-trust.

People can stop themselves long before their body does.

People should practice and train to grow rather than to fix what is wrong.

We get upset at bad shots because we think they are going to happen again.

A miss hit is an opportunity to evaluate your commitment.

Playfully swing like you do not care where the ball goes.

Our goal should be to focus on finding our own path to progress, rather than trying to master golf.

Past experiences lead to possibilities that lead to learning.

Stop any conscious inner self-talk so that you can experience what is happening.

Learning is not hitting good shots; it's knowing the cause.

When training, maybe the first questions should be

How have you been trying to improve?
What did you learn?
Did you have any fun?

CHAPTER FOUR
Insights into Core Knowledge

Golf's Basic Core Information

Golf's Physical Basics

Shaft Before Club Face

Golf Club Laws

Training the Club

Golf's Basic Core Information

Let's play with this idea; what a golfer should be doing with their golf club is determined by the conditions of the shot they are about to play, and the design of a golf club, and **not** some expert model, or a list of technical details. For hundreds of years golf clubs have been manufactured with two shaft angles.

(1) The shaft of a golf club is designed to angle up from the ground at more or less a 45° angle when the club is placed behind the ball at address.

(2) The shaft also is designed to be angled forward of the club's face. Each golf club in a set of fourteen clubs has a different face loft angle. The greater the loft angle, the shorter the length of shaft. For example, long shafted drivers can have less than ten degrees of loft, and the short-shafted wedges may have more than 60° of loft. Long-shafted, low-lofted clubs are used for long shots, while the shorter-shafted clubs with more loft are used for shorter-length shots. Each club is designed to fly the ball different distances and different heights that influence the bounce and roll of the ball on landing.

The basic core idea of an efficient golf stroke is to:

(1) swing the shaft of the club through impact parallel to the angle it occupied at address,

(2) with the shaft of the club swinging through impact before the club face.

In general (for a right-handed golfer) if the shaft is swinging over the original angle it occupied at address, and the club face is looking in the same direction, the golf ball will fly to the left. If the club shaft is swinging under the original angle it occupied at address, and the club face is looking in the same direction, the golf ball will fly to the right. In

general, when the club face gets to the ball before the shaft, the ball is impacted with less force than when the shaft swings through impact before the club face and club head. ***Shaft before club face through impact* is a useful visualization.**

Normally when the face of the club is angled in a different direction than the path the club head and shaft are swinging on, the golf ball will fly in either a hook or slice spin path. An open face at impact tends to create a slice spin while a closed face at impact tends to create a hook spin. There are as many ball flight variations as there are variations of the angle of the club face to the club head path at impact.

Golf clubs have left the factory with two shaft angles (1) up from the ground and (2) forward of the club's face for hundreds of years. We could say that most unwanted outcomes happen when the swing is redesigning these angles through impact. The shaft is either swinging through impact too high or too low, or **it is swinging through impact** just right for the shot at hand, with the shaft either passing the ball before or after the club face at impact. Said another way, the club head is either behind our hands or in front of our hands through impact, with the shaft either swinging parallel to the angle it occupied at address or it is not. **That is golf's basic core information.**

See clubs on page 54.

At the 2005 Byron Nelson Classic, Tiger Woods missed his first cut in 142 tournaments over seven years, which had amounted to the longest no-cut streak in the PGA Tour history. "I couldn't quite find where I needed to put the club to actually make a golf swing. I struggled warming up; I just didn't have it today."[17]

When a golf club is swinging efficiently, our body moves efficiently. What do you want the shaft, club face, and club head do for a the particular shot at hand? Some golfers feel that they swing the club by turning their bodies, and others by swinging their arms. What is important is to just swing the weight of the club. A thought shared by instructor Susan Berdoy Meyers is, "The stroke has a beginning and an ending with nothing in the middle."

From day one we all have been learning to use or interact in our environment. We learned what to do with a toothbrush; we didn't learn to use our hand and arm. We learned what to do with the handlebar of a bicycle, or a car's steering wheel; we didn't learn to use our arms. Children are not learning to use their bodies. They are learning what to do with the objects; which playfully trains body movements. When a golf club is doing what it should be doing for the shot being played, the golfer's body will be efficiently doing what it should be doing. The game of golf has what is referred to as its ball flight laws. I feel it would be a more efficient approach to learning golf to use what I call *Golf Club Laws*, or *what to do with the golf club's alignment through impact*, which creates different ball flight paths (side spin).

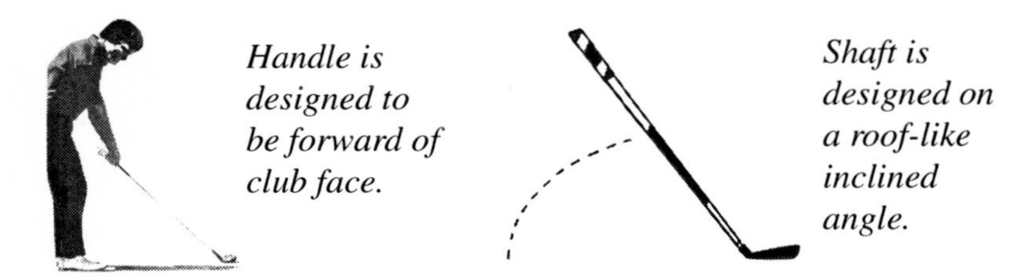

17 Brad Kearns, *How Tiger Does It*, pg 142

Golf's Physical Basics

The following is about "golf's physical basics." These basics are non-negotiable. They have been the same for every golfer dating back to when people first started to swing a club and play golf - long before any formal instruction was available. **Guidelines for swinging and playing really become self-evident when they are based on golf's physical basics.**

Golf's physical basics can help people who are not happy with their progress develop new insights and perceptions. They are not intended to tell anyone how to swing the club and play golf.

A list of basics is always useful to use when learning to improve anything, including one's golf. The question becomes, whose list of basics is going to be used? Some golfers go from tip to tip where there is little common ground and where there are disagreements over what should be on a list of basics.

My suggestion is to use a list of golf's physical basics. It is a list that always has common ground and avoids disagreements.

There was no formal golf instruction information available hundreds of years ago, but from day one:

- The purpose of the game has always been to enjoy ourselves as we learn to influence both the distance and direction of ball flight.
- Golf has always been played with a stick, a ball, and on an ever changing field of play.
- The golf club has always had a head, club face, and shaft, with all three determining ball flight.
- A golf club has always been designed with its handle end angled forward of the club face, and with the shaft angled up from the ground on a roof-like, inclined angle.
- Golfers have always stood inside the ball and target line.

- The motion of the swing has always had some source of power. This motion has always had some level of balance and timing.
- Golfers have always had hands, arms, and bodies.

I do not believe anything has been overlooked. These elements have all been the same from day one. When looking to improve one's influence over the flight of the ball, any effective approach can be founded on elements listed above, and golf's physical basics listed below.

Golf's Five Physical Basics:

(1) The design of the club, i.e., the angles of a shaft, club face, and head.

(2) Golfers stand inside the ball and target line.

(3) The ballistic properties of the compressible ball.

(4) The elements of balance and time.

(5) The field of play and ever-changing playing conditions.

This may seem like a short list, especially when compared to all the information that is available to golfers today. But all basic requirements of an effective swing and playing the game are based on golf's physical basics.

Through Impact:

- The club is either on-plane, or it is not.
- The club head mass is either behind the grip, or it is not.
- The ball is either compressed, or it is not.
- The swing has efficient timing and balance, or it does not.
- The player has adapted his stance and swing motion to the shot at hand, or they have not.

Let me say that again. **All the basic elements of an effective swing and playing the game are based on golf's physical basics.** The origin of these basics is not someone's opinion. Nature's truth simply knows no other possibilities. Unless the design angles of the club, ballistic properties of the ball, the human form, the field of play, or the principles of motion and force change, these physical basics seem to be non-negotiable and are the foundation of good golf.

The search for solutions leads to finding the tools for solutions. Golf's physical basics are the tools for an effective swing and playing the game.

Golfers who make progress and experience long-term learning, are able to evaluate the current golf course environment, utilize golf's physical basics and adapt their swing with a process called "reverse engineering." Engineering builds to create; on the other hand, reverse engineering adapts to environments.

In 1993, I wrote and compiled *Building and Improving Your Golf Mind, Golf Body, Golf Swing.* In hindsight I would have titled the book *Adapting to Improve Your Golf Mind, Golf Body, Golf Swing.*

People who make progress with golf have learned the value of adapting golf's physical basics with reverse engineering principles for the shot about to be played (which is the most useful swing model). The body humans occupy today was developed over millions of years using reverse engineering and natural selection to adapt every gene in the body to the ever changing environment (good golfers also adapt).

Shaft Before Club Face

There is a good chance that many questions about inconsistent golf could be satisfied with accurate insights into the principle of shaft before club face through impact. For some golfers these insights will be profound for accomplishing a powerful on-line ball flight.

When the shaft of the golf club is not traveling through impact before the club face, there is a good chance golfers will not be happy with the results of their swing. There are some short game and other specialty shots that are an exception to this principle of shaft-before-club face (when the most efficient way to play the shot at hand would be to let the club face pass the shaft).

Generally, the concept of swinging the shaft of a golf club through impact before the club face answers many questions about inconsistent ball flight from fairways and tees. Some golfers may not realize that golf club shafts are designed on angles that come up from the ground angled forward of the club face. The shaft is designed to be leaning forward, with the grip end in front of the club face. For most shots in golf, golfers should be swinging the club through impact - *shaft before club face!* It may help improve inconsistencies to focus more on swinging the entire shaft (all 34" to 44", depending on the club) through impact before the club face, rather than focusing on the club head.

Other visualizations that may help golfers accomplish the all-important principle of shaft before club face through impact are:

Have the feeling that your hands, your right shoulder (right handed golfers), and the club shaft are all swinging down plane through impact at the same pace or rate of motion.

Try replacing the often-used swing thought of "one and two" with the feeling of a long one count from start to finish. Feel the swing that has the same pace from start to finish.

"Shaft before club head" is a fundamental that often gets overlooked by golfers who are focusing on how to move their bodies.

I have found it more useful to focus on what you want to do with the golf club's shaft, head, and face (which depends on the shot at hand), than focusing on how to move one's body. By avoiding tips from your well-meaning friends about how to move your body (tips that are always changing), you can accomplish several fundamentals of consistent golf.

Training the Club's Three Elements

A golf club will not move until the golfer's body parts move first. Some approaches for helping golfers improve tell golfers how to move their bodies. While it is true that a golf club does react to the body's moving parts, when it comes to long-term learning, a stronger case can be made for golfers learning how the club's head, face, and shaft should be aligned through impact for the shot at hand. Again, **I have found it is more useful to know what to do with the club, than trying to focus on how to move body parts**.

A golf club has three elements: its club face, club head, and shaft, and it helps to stay aware of these three elements.

Golfers can work on their swing and game in a variety of ways. I would suggest using training time to discover efficient alignments of the golf club's three elements (club face, head and shaft) for the shot at hand. **When developing your game and swing, pick one (face, head or shaft) at a time to be aware of, not tips from your friends.**

My suggestion: do not try to learn how to move your body per se, but become aware of, and learn the required alignments of the shaft, club face, and club head through impact. Where you want the shaft, club head, and club face at impact for the shot at hand is a more useful focus than thinking about moving body parts.

- Was the club face open or closed at impact? Did the ball start right or left?
- Was the club face behind my hands or ahead of them? Was impact weak or solid?
- Was the shaft above, below, or one the same lie angle it occupied at address through impact? Did the ball fly left, right, or straight?
- Where was the shaft pointing at the top of the swing? Did the ball have any side spin in flight?

Keep in mind that ball flight is the direct result of speed and how the club's three elements are aligned through impact. Nature's truths do not know any other possibilities.

Some general observations about the design of a club are that when the shaft and swing forces are not parallel to the angle the shaft occupied at address through impact, it causes a ball flight that is not straight.

Every desired ball flight has a corresponding alignment and path of club face, head, and shaft for the shot at hand. When players are aware of the alignments of a club's three elements through impact it is possible to build an effective swing.

Let's Review!

Through Impact: When the face of the club is either open or closed to the club head path, side spin is increased.

An OPEN club face with the club head coming to the ball from outside the target line increases left-to-right side spin.

A CLOSED club face with the club head coming from inside the target line increases right-to-left side spin.

Through Impact: When the face of the club is facing in the same direction as the club head is traveling; (Both flights without side spin)

An **out-to-in path** PULLS the ball off line to the left.

An **in-to-out path** PUSHES the ball off line to the right.

When the player swings the club through impact without any changes to its original angles, the shaft, club head, and club face are all said to be on plane (with the club face behind the grip end), normally giving the player an efficient application and alignment of force.

When players intentionally alter one or more of the original design angles through impact, they can intentionally alter the application of force and the flight of the ball, making it go high or low, or give the ball a left or right to left side spin for the shot at hand.

When the original design angles are changing unintentionally through impact, they produce thin and fat shots. Shots can also go higher or lower, hooking and slicing out of control unintentionally - all caused by the original design angles of the club going through impact unintentionally out of control, producing a misapplication of force.

Awareness of golf club alignments is an initial step to making progress.

Golf Club Laws

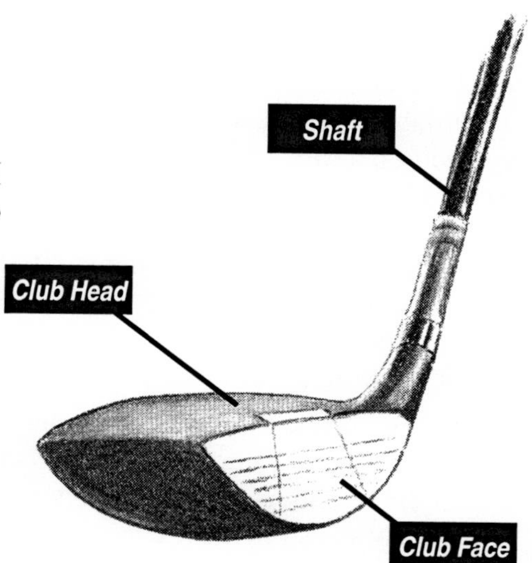

The game of golf has what is referred to as its ball flight laws. I have found using what I call ***Golf Club Laws***[18] - what to do with the three components of a golf club through impact to create different ball flights - to be a more efficient approach for learning to play the game than focusing on how to move one's body.

The Club

Any efforts to build an effective golf swing will be less than they could be when the design angles of the golf club are not taken into consideration is the message here.

Golfers can work on their swing and game in a variety of ways, but I would like to suggest using your training time to learn the alignments of a golf club's club face, head, and shaft for the shot you want to make. Develop a swing using the 3 elements the club was designed with, not tips from your friends.

In 1919 Harry Vardon said, *"The best advice I can give — you must obey the club and what the club wants you to do, letting results be natural."*

In 1930, Bobby Jones, a champion golfer, who may have been the best of his time, said *"Golfers should first and most importantly learn how the club face and the ball interact at impact. No one can play good golf until they know all the many ways a ball can be expected to react when struck in different ways."*

---

18 "Golf Club Laws" is a trademark of Learning Golf Inc.

When working on your game and swing, you can pick one (face, head or shaft) at a time to be aware of. It is not difficult to learn where and what the club head, club face and shaft are doing at impact. Just let yourself be aware, and don't fill your mind with swing tips. Becoming aware of the club's 3 elements is a much easier skill to learn than learning how to type reasonably well, **much easier**! There are only three elements (face, head, and shaft to be aware of) and not the 50+ keys that are on most modern computer keyboards to learn. I know a 6 year olds who are aware of what the club face, club head, and shaft are doing through impact more often than not.

When high school students or adults go to driving education classes, a general description of what they intend to do is: learn to drive. When driver education is looked at from a different point of view, we can clearly see students are learning to influence a steering wheel, a gas and brake pedal. When students learn to influence these three elements of a car they are developing a unconscious foundation for driving a car.

Driving a car is really the end result of learning to influence a steering wheel, a gas, and brake pedal. Just as an effective golf swing is clearly the end product of learning to influence the shaft, face, and head of a golf club. My suggestion is do not try to learn the golf swing per se, but become aware of and learn the required **alignments of shaft, club face, and club head at impact** for the shot at hand. Be engaged with what you want. The end product then becomes a golf swing with effective alignment and application of force, just as learning to influence a steering wheel, gas and brake pedal is the foundation for improving driving skills.

I suggest staying away from swing thoughts and tips from your friends, and become more open and unconsciously aware of golf ball laws when training and practicing.

- Was the club face open or closed at impact?
- Was the club face behind my hands or ahead of them?
- Was the shaft above, below, or on the same lie angle it was on at address through impact?

Your golf club laws can give you the answers to all these and similar questions (nature knows no other possibilities) Did the ball start right or left? Did the ball have any side spin? Was impact solid or weak? Did the ball fly to high or two low? It's the rules for the club that produce ball fight.

Some general observations about the design of a club are as follows:

Keep in mind every desired ball flight (high, low, left, right, etc.) has a corresponding alignment and path of club face, head, and shaft that must be taken into consideration for the shot at hand before the player swings. **After players are aware of impact alignments for the club's three elements that it is possible to build an effective swing.** Train so you learn to be unconsciously aware of where the club face, head, and shaft are at impact. (For example, a sand shot requires different alignments than the driver swing. Players should be previewing *seeing* and *feeling* impact alignments before they start their swing.)

It is quite possible no one has ever asked you to become aware of the club face, head, and shaft before. But this **is a real key to an efficient swing**! Let me ask, *If we do not know where club face, head and shaft are and what they are doing, how can we change our flight?* Becoming aware of current alignments and angles is the first step to progress.

Any guidelines for golf swings that can produce effective impact force and alignments for the shot we are playing have the design of the club at their foundation.

CHAPTER FIVE
Swing Model

Consistency, Maybe No!

Playing golf requires a golf swing that can make adjustments for different circumstances every time a golfer swings. I seriously question the value of trying to consistently copy the technical details of an efficient swing because every swing is made under different conditions from the ones a player will have in the future.

Golfers who are working on developing a consistent swing may want to re-think this modeling/copying approach. Every swing is, and has to be, different. No swing made in the past was exactly the same, and no swing made in the future will be the same. A flexible, portable swing style, one that can playfully adjust to the changing conditions during a round of golf, would be a more useful goal than trying to make a consistent swing. **To perform the specific, we should be educated in variety.**

Tiger Woods - "You have to make adjustments each and every day, from shot to shot. All the things I've experienced just got put into my file. I've been on tour 12 years, each and every day you feel a little bit different and you have to make slight adjustments to hit the shot you want to hit. It is just experiences and you can learn from them. I guarantee you 10 years from now that I'll be a hell of a lot better with my course management than I am now, just because of that many years of experience." (March 22, 2008, at Doral Country Club after 3rd WGC-CA championship)

I once had a famous tour professional say to me, "Michael, I'm working on making my swing more consistent." I asked, "Why? Every swing you will make in the future will have to be adjusted to the dissimilar conditions of play." **A flexible, portable swing style developed with a playful approach in random, ever changing environments will pay more dividends than working on trying to make a swing consistent.**

In playing-to-learn environments ***the aim is to playfully learn to be consistently creative***. Playing-to-learn creatively (not consistently) is a brain compatible approach for making progress. The skills that consistently produce workable outcomes are learned and developed under ever changing conditions, by playfully training with a variety of approaches. The suggestion Silvia A. Bunge, Ph.D. (University of California at Berkeley) makes is, "To be fully engaged when there are novel challenges, unfamiliar contexts, difficult choices, and distractions." A consistent mind-set and consistent emotions with a consistently creative golf swing is the aim of a playful approach to learning golf.

Rethinking the Use of Drills and Expert Models

For years, many people have believed the fastest most productive way to learn tasks was to rehearse and repeat them over and over using drills and expert models. Research done by Dr. Langer of Harvard, and many other leaders in education now show there are some problems with this long held approach. The approach of repeating and repeating does not leave much room for self-discovery and rethinking information. Studies now show there are more effective ways of mastering skills. Dr. Langer calls it "mindful learning" (as opposed to mindless), and points out that long-term learning requires much more than drills founded on memorization, repetition, and rote. Conventional learning (drills) depends on automatic behavior, which stifles creativity and undermines self-esteem as individuals struggle and often fail to learn techniques adequately with a mindless drill approach.

Drills

Studies show that using drills leads to boring, mindless, non-focused training sessions that leave people with little or no insights into the skill they are trying to learn. Using a repeating unthinking manor to learn basics can almost guarantee mediocrity.

To explain why repetitive golf drills tend to be ineffective, Geoff Ogilvy (2006 US Open Champion) said, "It is like throwing pebbles in a bucket. At some point it gets boring and you lose your feel."[19]

Drills are normally based on **how-to** directions that are not giving individuals the opportunity to gain insights and options they did not have in the past. Expert golfers become experts by developing various ways to use the very basics some golfers are trying to improve with mindless repetitions. In the October 2008 issue of *Golf Digest* magazine Arnold Palmer said, "What sets outstanding players apart is the ability to *vary* the speed of the club head, and *adjust* the swing path and club face to hit little draws and fades and *alter* the trajectory of the ball flight." Palmer used the words vary, adjust and alter when referring to touch or feel, then asked, "How do you teach that?" (meaning you can't teach it!). Palmer went on to say, "Using my sense of feel (adjusting) came by accident, it takes time for your brain to adapt."

The suggestion here is with a play-to-learn approach to progress the skills of adjusting and adapting your feel and touch are enhanced randomly, without drills, how-to directions, or a list of details from a perceived expert.

Studies show that learning happens best when skills are performed when conditions are not static - i.e., golfers are never faced with the exact same shot or conditions, with tour players adjusting their basic skills in every kind of context.

---

19 *Sports Illustrated* magazine, June 12, 2007

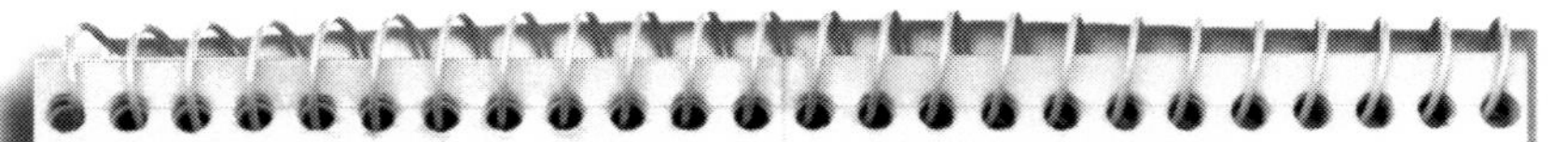

Note: Repetition can create mediocre skills, with most people not experiencing (self-discovery) thinking beyond the information they have been given. When we are learning like robots, rehearsing over and over, it deprives students of maximizing their full potential to learn the application of skills in ever changing situations. Players never learn how to use their own personal and unique physical skills, mental abilities, and personalities to their fullest from how-to lists, and drills.

Note: Simply memorizing the execution of information will not lead to long-term learning, but awareness and self-directed learning can.

Using a general, just in the ball park concept of a task (no details) and moving away from the obsessions of trying to get it right in drills, brings on the joy of learning. Fear of negative evaluation can take the fun out of anything. For example, Dr. Langer points out that if we were rated on how fast we completed crossword puzzles, how much enjoyment would we actually get from doing them. I suggest, when lost for a word having to search in different places for ideas, often requires the mind to do some work that one feels good about when the answer is found. Looking and finding really can be more fun and rewarding ***(Yes, I found it!)*** than immediately knowing what word the puzzle is looking for.

When learners stop judging themselves when doing drills and become more involved in the whole experience of learning through awareness and self-help, pleasure and productivity become partners on the path to long-term progress. **I know asking golfers who are learning to move away from using drills is controversial, but it's a decision that studies (and my experiences) show will lead to long-term learning.**

Churchland's Discovery on Repetition

12:47 December 2006, *NewScientist.com* news service, *New Scientist* staff and AFP

Endless hours spent perfecting your golf swing or basketball shot could be a waste of time, according to a new study, which shows that practice does not always make perfect.

Mark Churchland and colleagues at Stanford University in California, US, made the discovery after training subjects to repeat a simple reaching task thousands of times.

"The nervous system was not designed to do the same thing over and over again," says Churchland, whose team investigated the way the brain plans and calculates motion.

The team showed the subjects a colored spot and rewarded them for reaching out to touch it at different speeds. During the exercise, they monitored the promoter cortex of the subjects' brains, which is the region responsible for movement planning, and tracked the speed of the resulting motion.

Over the course of thousands of reaches, the subjects rarely moved with exactly the same speed. Small variations in reach speed followed by small variations in brain activity during movement planning, the researchers said.

Conventional Wisdom

Contrary to conventional wisdom that movement variability is caused by muscle activity, Churchland's team found that neural activity accounts for about half the variations. In other words, training muscles to perform a certain way through practice, such as countless hours teeing off or shooting a basketball, will not produce the same shot every time because the brain's behavior is inconsistent.

After an initial training period, the subjects reach accuracy did not improve over time, suggesting that lots of practice can only improve movement control so much, said team member Krishna Shenoy.

The researchers speculate that humans and animals evolved with this "improvisational style" in response to the predator-prey dynamic where predators never catch and kill prey in exactly the same conditions.

"Premium athletes quest for consistency is a stark contrast to the way we evolved through history," Shenoy said.

*For more insights see the essay **Training Time on Tasks** in the **Extra Credit** section.*

Expert Models

After years of studies Professor Gibson F. Dardon of Radford University and many others in the field of motor learning now point to evidence that the use of expert models **only encourages imitation** (much of the following information is based on their work).

When learning a motion (i.e., tennis or golf swing motions) a past and popular notion has been to watch an expert model. This was thought to be a good representation of what to do, and also a comparison for changing unworkable habits. It has been said the more frequent learners see expert models the stronger the mental blueprint of the model would be, hopefully, translating into increased abilities to perform and change unworkable motions. As we know, coaches from many sports have supported the use of expert models for years.

Expert models often do not guide learning into retention of the skills (or rules of motion) needed to perform in ever-changing real-life conditions and situations. Schmidt (1991) and Magill (1993) point out that motor skill learning is largely rule learning.

Typically expert models have provided demonstrations of motion we trust people will be able to copy. In fact there are any number of popular video instruction systems that compare expert models to a learners motion. **This form of training leads to a performance that is called a conditioned reflex** (Lee, et al., 1994, pg 330). With the ever-changing conditions playing golf can present, golfers would be better served if they developed some creative skills so they could make adjustments for the shot at hand. **Developing a "conditioned reflex"**

using drills to copy expert models is not the most useful learning strategy for learning to play golf.

Today there is evidence that supports using variable training (i.e., different speeds, swing sizes, paths, and club face alignments) in a golf swing motion does in fact promote more effective learning of rules of a motion. These rules and their own feel of principles of motion help people learn **cause and effect** of motion patterns. The increased variety during a training session can result in a stronger memory of the basic skills needed to influence the club head, club face and shaft through impact.

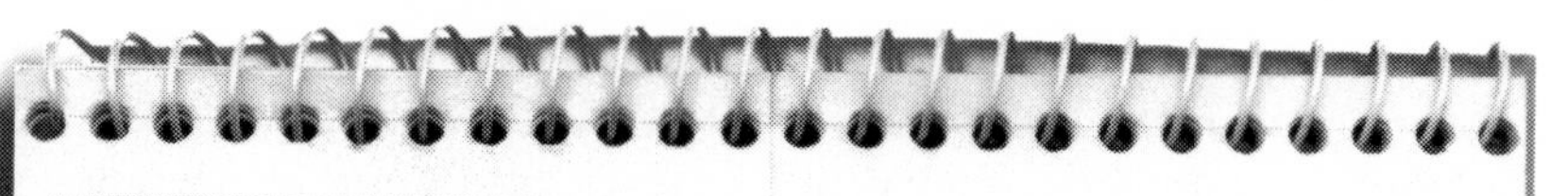

Note: Repeating an error-free performance (i.e., standing in some swing ring, swinging over and over) imitating an expert model appears to ignore what we now know about learning motions (Mangill 1993, Lee, et al., 1994) — Errorless practice and repetition are poor learning strategies. **After a skill has been learned, repeating it over and over can have some value to highly skilled performers, but not for most learners.** Apparently there is real value in missing a foul shot, or missing a serve in tennis, or missing a shot in golf (when it is not criticized or judged.) "Players learn from their mistakes," "Players have to learn what it takes to win," "I must keep putting myself in position to win before I learn what it takes to win,"[20] are all familiar statements sports announcers and players make.

Workable and unworkable actions (both mental and physical) must be experienced for long-term learning to take hold. A player's brain and feel system must become educated to a variety of motions. **Becoming aware of the differences in workable and unworkable motion is the first stage of long-term retention of any skill.** Jack Nicklaus said that during his practice he devotes some of his time to

20 Jack Nicklaus quote

making incorrect swings so he can feel the difference between correct and incorrect swing dynamics.[21]

Golfers looking for long-term retention of skills should avoid learning a task under false pretenses (static conditions). Real life performance conditions require problem solving skills and adjustments strategies. If golfers must train and practice on a range I suggest making believe you are playing holes, or change clubs after each swing, as you change targets and size of swings. **This kind of variation in training is more useful for long-term learning than imitating expert models using a how-to list.**

Golfers who want to improve should first educate themselves about the nature of learning and not look for immediate success that often leaves as quickly as they arrived. **Learning should be seen as problem solving (i.e., seeing options).** Seeing options or problem solving often does not lead to increased levels of performance during practice. However, since skill development is internal at first and therefore invisible, evidence of a learning transfer can show up at any time. People should understand the difference in temporary effects of practice and long-term retention of skills, or we could say, **the difference in trying to fix a habit and learning a new habit**.

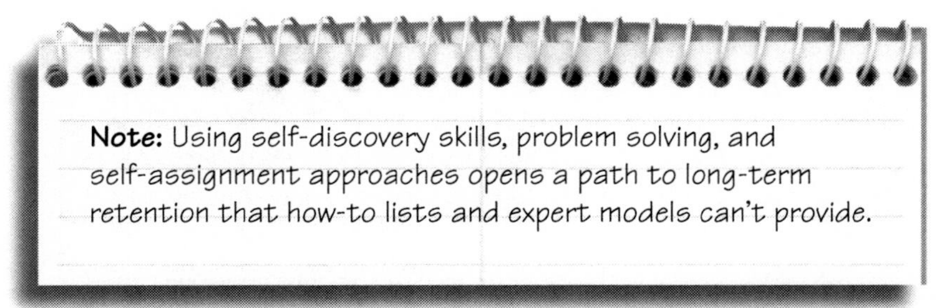

Learning Models

People must believe they can achieve a model level of performance. Often when expert models are used, self-confidence can be damaged. Without some level of confidence progress for anyone is difficult. Studies now suggest using a **learning model** (non expert), where people will be encouraged by a model that takes into consideration the strengths and limitations of the individual learner. **Any pressure**

21 Jack Nicklaus, *The Impact Zone*, pg 199

to do it like the expert can prevent some people from discovering what can work best for them. Trying to copy an expert model can stop people from exploring different feels for being on-plane for example, and overlooks the power of self-discovery and awareness.

Learning models by their nature are variable models, and have been found to be very beneficial for long-term learning (Schmidt 1991). **It is now believed when people become more aware in general non-specific terms** (i.e., aware of on or off-plane swing motion, aware of a club head that is behind the player's hands through impact, and a club head that is not; aware of what is workable balancing and what is not; aware of workable swing timing and what is not; of workable posture and alignment), **it's more useful than trying to imitate an expert model**. An expert model can get ones attention and may even increase motivation, but with respect to the process of learning or thinking about the skill, **expert models fall short when compared to general descriptions and self-discovery**.

It is more useful for people to sense personal accurate feedback about **their** own performance than to have information from an **expert model**. Personal feedback enhances motivation and guides learners away from trying for results with their ball flight, into observations about motion or process of learning. Accurate immediate feedback (using mirrors and ball flight) can allow people to become aware of their golf club motion. It seems **expert models** require accuracy that at times is beyond the skill level of some learners, lowering self-confidence.

Note: A cutting-edge hypothesis points out, the most effective demonstration (model) seems to be one that is only slightly above the learner's current skill level, promoting persistence and self-esteem during learning (McCullagh and Caird, 1990). It seems golfers would be better off if their personal perspective was more or less just in the "Ball Park," and not necessarily a perfect picture.

Using a non-specific learning model can be a more effective method for allowing people to become skillful at their current level, especially when combined with accurate and immediate feedback.

Several studies question the need to give people explicit information on how to execute motor skills (Rink 1994). People only need general information about appropriate movement patterns to reach the goal of very accurate or explicit patterns of motion. Several recent studies suggest observing a learning model (a non-specific generalization) is more effective than using an expert model. **Allowing people to explore possible solutions is a critical aspect of the learning process.** From this view **expert models** may indeed restrict learning.

It may be difficult for many of us who have used expert models (including myself) in the past to believe by replacing the expert model with a learning model, long term learning will be enhanced. But I can say from experience working with general information rather than very specific details enhances learning. **Based on what is now known about learning, golfers should consider moving away from expert models into using a learning model.** You may want very specific results and alignments, and progress in this direction is possible for any golfer.

More About Expert Models vs. Learning Models

Studies from the field of cognitive science have shown that any pressure to get it right or do it like an expert creates stress related emotions that prevent individuals from learning what can work best for them. Trying to copy an expert model can also produce what could be called artificial intelligence or information void of personal insights from one's own curiosity and imagination.

Unfortunately, golf orientation often disorients and fragments progress when expert models are being used. Two examples:

(1) Golfers viewing recorded images of their swing with an instructor who is pointing out mistakes and drawing lines over their swing motion.

(2) Golfers who have their swing motion compared to some expert's swing motion on a split screen. These are not pro-active approaches to learning.

The above are just two examples of how expert models can create stress-related emotions that fragment learning. Scientists now know a great deal about how the brain encodes long-term learning. Learning environments and learning opportunities must be free of the kind of stress that fragments learning in order to be effective.

Learning models are designed to be general in nature, offering just-in-the-ball-park descriptions of events. Expert models are exact, and are normally being used to try to fix poor outcomes. On the other hand learning models are not trying to fix poor habits, they are offering a *pro-active* learning experience that helps individuals invent and find their own best way, while using a general non-specific concept. **Keep in mind that information that is geared for helping someone is not as valuable as information that's geared for helping someone to help him or herself.** When it comes to long term learning trying to fix a poor habit is less effective than a proactive focus on a positive image of what-to-do. Studies show attempts to *fix* do not lead to learning that lasts, but staying engaged with *what*-to-do can.

Learning models promote interacting with ever-changing environments (active learning), and an interest in problem-solving (finding options) with personal insights. On the other hand, expert models promote passive learning (following directions), memorization and superficial non-personal decoding. **Following directions does not fully engage the higher cortex of the brain where learning takes place.**

Golf is a game of adjustments and recovery while using reasoning and deduction skills. Learning models are variable models that can birth the kind of flexible knowledge and portable skills needed for interacting in the ever-changing environments that playing golf presents. Learning models also give individuals the opportunity to make personal choices, said to be the most empowering opportunity individuals can be given.

I played basketball in high school and college, playing with more than a few future All-Americans and NBA players, and none of us tried to copy an expert model to learn the skills of shooting, dribbling, passing, or running. Everyone was aware that the basketball had to go up, because the net was up (core knowledge). We focused on *what* to do, not *how* to do it. Over time, any personal how-to details of these skills just filled in through the trial and feedback of self-discovery learning. In a learning-developing environment there is no failure, only feedback, to be used as reference points in the future. These learning environments offer the opportunity to mimic; they are not asking individuals to produce exact copies.

Ever-Changing Details

The increasing and continuing volume of micromanaged details found in golf instruction has created a cycle of division between the nature of the learning process and making progress at an acceptable rate. When individuals are not pleased with their pace of progress, often it is all the details in some new theory that are problematic. The nature of long-term learning wants to use general, just-in-the-ballpark concepts, not a list of details.

The view here is that being more child like using a self-discovery approach will shed more light on learning than a long list of details. Child-like self-discovery is grounded in personal insights and *being* naturally curious. **It is a misleading belief that filling up the gaps in ones information base about moving our body and club is crucial for meaningful progress to take hold.** This belief should be rethought. We do not need a degree in cognitive science (just a different view) to gain a mind share into the value of going back to the roots of the learning process found in self-discovery and self-assessment. Mark Twain said, "A man cannot be comfortable without his own approval." A self-assessment approach to progress provides an effective self-reinforcing quality to learning and *being* one's self.

It has been said that scientists like to believe they will leave the world better than they found it. I'm sure educators, parents, coaches, and employers have similar feelings when they are giving advice. It has also been said that in science you often learn that the simplest answer is the best answer. This insight is sometimes lost in the world of high tech read outs and lists of intellectually interesting details about the golf swing, both of which are not brain compatible for *being* a long term learner.

Moving beyond a battlefield of detailed information and high tech readouts can be a galvanizing force which restores our connection to the nature of the learning process and fully turning on our cognitive light. **Pictures (without words), feels (without judgments), and past experiences (indirect perception) stored in our subconscious are all elements of the nature of the learning process.** A need to use a list of details is an attempt to passively induce progress, rather than being actively self-producing with the kind of intrinsic, creative, self-learning that fires up a startlingly efficient imagination. While being creative, flexible knowledge and portable skills are at the core of the nature of learning.

"If the person is acting on the expectations or values of others, if he acts to please or be approved of, if he does anything which violates his own nature or integrity, there can be no true or significant learning experience." Clark E. Moustakas[22]

A brain compatible approach to progress self-builds a community of personal experiences, rather than just looking for an exit strategy for a poor outcome from an outside source. **It's by embracing the experience of a poor outcome without trying to fix it, that you can find where the answer lies.** The answer always lies in the outcomes of our workable and unworkable interactions with the conditions of the environment.

The Past and Present

Beyond the hope of progress, what else could make approaches to learning more inviting? Individuals who are learning should have

22 Clark Moustakas, *Teaching as Learning*, pg 12

more than just the hope of progress - they should be aware that they are designed to learn without consciously trying. While this may be a counter intuitive insight, it is an accurate one about how past experiences are indirect preparation for future interactions with our environment. When the human brain has a new experience, or is taking in new information, it unconsciously and immediately cross-links, clusters, indexes, analyzes, remixes, and reassembles that information and simultaneously mixes it with our past experience through the steps of parallel processing.

Parallel processing is an unconscious act (a survivor skill) that sees patterns and relationships in our interactions in the now and simultaneously links this information to both related and unrelated past experiences we have had. This unconscious connection of past and present patterns and relationships seems to be essential to long-term learning.

Studies into the nature of learning show that learning directly from our experiences is not biologically possible (learning is a dynamic, organic biological process). Learning or developmental learning occurs when the patterns and relationships in what is taking place in the present are linked to past experience stored in our subconscious. This connection is mostly an unconscious event that occurs without trying.

Studies show that the conscious mind is not given important learning assignments because it has no past experiences available to help guide decisions. We could say up to 95% of what human beings do is influenced by our subconscious, where past experiences are stored as reference points for guiding future decisions.

The human brain is not designed to operate like a camera that is taking one picture at a time. The brain operates more like a committee that has all its members giving input into the decisions and choices being made. All of a human being's past experiences have their unconscious say and influence to some degree (large or small) what we are doing in the present.

Real or developmental learning is a transforming experience based on the unconscious mental links that find and tag onto past experiences stored in the brain. The steps and stages individuals go through during a new learning experience are not separated from prior experiences when long term learning is taking hold.

When new learning experiences take hold, they are supported by links to the database that past personal experiences have been created through what is referred to as active learning. In active learning environments, the acts of parallel processing travel from one past experience to the next, supporting the kind of learning that lasts. The patterns and relationships in past experiences when linked or parallel to experiences in the present are supporting the brain's ability to learn without consciously trying.

Search engines accomplish the linking process when they pull together collective intelligence. In our brain we could say that what is going on is a community activity, or group decisions about a topic from a collective point of view.

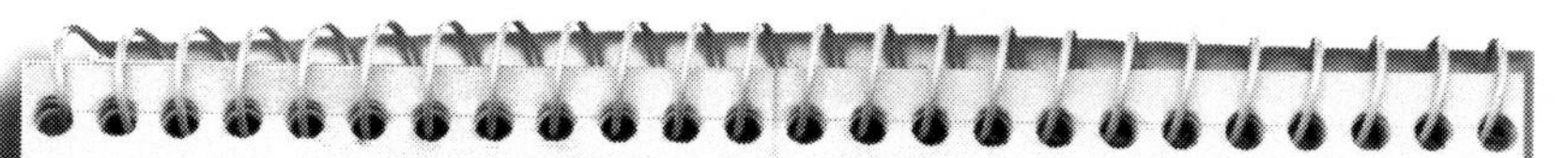

Note: Any original creations are developed from a collection of interconnected ideas and actions from past experiences. The brain could be seen as operating in a culture of unconscious interactions that participate in rounding up the past, to make experiences in the present deeper and richer, thereby providing more meaningful insights for making sense of the present.

The brain is normally seen as a discovery tool operating in the present, but the reality that acts of learning are integrated unconsciously with past experiences is often overlooked. Successful ideas and actions are woven from many ideas and other experiences, exposing the reality that the past and present are inseparable. **Human beings are designed to succeed, thrive and survive, not to fail.** Said another way, we are designed to be influenced by our past experiences acting as unconscious reference points for successfully guiding future interactions with our environment.

When we are actively engaged with the environment, our subconscious has the ability to influence and guide our thoughts and actions in the present. We could say that when we are actively engaged there is little we do or think about that is actually a first time experience. Our thoughts and actions in the present are being guided by the indirect preparation of past experiences stored in our subconscious. Staying actively engaged, is normally referred to as being in the present, but in reality our experiences and acts of parallel processing help what is going on in the present. **Play with the idea that staying engaged is an act of letting in, while focusing is an act of seeking or trying that can fragment progress.**

There is Little You Must Do, Only Things You Can Do.

What is being said here is that golf is a game to be played, and not a subject to be taught.

The view here is do not try to copy the style of any one particular player. When learning and developing swings and games golfers should keep their own identity. On both the PGA Tour and the LPGA Tour there are many golfers with highly personal swing styles.

Golfers who are using a swing that is unusual may have what others would call some poor habits. But every golfer at every level, from new to experienced, professional to amateur, have poor habits that at times produce some unwanted outcomes. Normally, experienced golfers are aware of what may be their poor habits and see the unwanted outcomes as feedback for future use rather than seeing poor outcomes as failure. These poor habits can be used as sign posts for doing something different instead of trying to *fix* them. According to studies from the science of learning, staying engaged with what you want to do with the golf club for the shot at hand is more useful for making progress than trying to change poor habits. **Staying engaged with what you want to do is a positive approach to making progress, while fixing is a negative approach.**

Golf is not so much a game of "must-dos" as it is a game of adjustments and discoveries gained through self-discovery and self-assessment. If you want to hold the club in a particular way, just make sure your swing, posture, ball location and alignment fit the grip you want to use. Every professional golfer has a grip style that is different or unique.

If you want to stand to the ball in a particular way, just make sure your grip and swing style fit with the way you are standing to the ball for the shot you want to hit. (Every professional golfer has their own way of standing to the ball.)

If you want your alignment to be a particular way, just make sure your grip and type of shot you want to hit fit that alignment.

I could go on, but keep in mind there are more things you can do, then you must do.

A Speech by Clark McKowern

Playful Thinking

The following are highlights from a graduation address that Clark McKowern (author of *Teaching Human Beings*) gave to graduates of Diablo Valley College in Pleasant Hill, California. His title: "Things we forget to tell you." This speech contains insights into the process of learning anything, even golf.

> *Your mind is a connecting organ. Your mind loves to make connections. If it gets into a confusing situation, it's going to find some way to get rid of that confusion. So it's quite natural for you to solve problems. That's what I want to talk with you about tonight.*
>
> *I want to get it on the record that every human being in the audience is very smart. The neocortex, the new brain can do amazing, unbelievably complex things. In fact, when you were born, you were using it expertly maybe better than when you were in college. You taught yourself a language. We have plenty of research to show that nobody else did that for you. You're an expert.*

The point is that you don't have to know consciously how to do it. It's child's play. The neocortex, that new brain, it's your sand box. It's part of the brain that does not speak a language, but it does just fine; it functions beautifully without your conscious knowledge. You don't have to know how it works, but you do have to trust that it will work for you.

The neocortex will not give your conscious mind wonderful solutions if it's mistreated. When mistreated it won't communicate. It takes instructions, not from the conscious mind, but from our emotions. If your emotions don't give its OK, your neocortex malfunctions. It won't know what to do, and whatever it does won't feel right. There is a door between your conscious mind and the unconscious. If you try hard to think, the door remains shut.

Your brain will function well only when it is fired by your enthusiasm, your joy, your pleasure. That means you have to find out how to be full of joy under all circumstances. When you were a kid, that part of yourself directed all your activities. Know that when you are at your top level of performance, you behave exactly like you did when you were "playing," playing at language, playing at walking, playing in your neocortex. If subjects or managing your life seems hard for you, it simply means you are probably trying to use your new brain in an unnatural way. If you use it the same way as you did when you were a little kid, you can solve problems effortlessly.

On the other hand, if you have to make yourself do something, it's a clear signal to stop and try another way that's not so grouchy or grumpy.

The natural way is almost upside down from what we have been led to believe. We are taught to work hard at our studies on solving problems, but that is not the way our brains work best. The brain works best when it is in a playful mood. ***We can use our conscious minds to set up problems, but we have to get playful if we want to solve them.***

The truth is that great thinkers, the great artists, the great scientists of the world have treated their work as if it were play. They have been, you might say, irresponsible, but that is not to say they haven't done things that turned out to be valuable to the human race. But while they were thinking, they could not be filled with effort. So it is the opposite of what we are used to hearing. That is something you need to know about.

While you are thinking, while you are trying to solve problems, you cannot be working at them; you can only be having a good time, like a kid in a sandbox. If you want to make those things become a reality, and your self-play at its best, you will get much better results. If you want to discover, and want to use your mind really well, you must be playful, joyous, and irresponsible. If you can remember these things about yourself, you will be in great shape.

1 Moustakas, Clark, *The Authentic Teacher*

2 Moustakas, Clark, *Personal Growth: The Struggle for Identity and Human Values*

CHAPTER SIX
The Lesson Experience

Before Instruction

First, prior to taking a lesson, it helps to realize that playing a good game of golf is an acquirable skill. Golf is no different than learning how to type, draw, or play a musical instrument. Like all acquirable skills, golf can be LEARNED in playful steps and stages. But, for some reason, when it comes to learning or improving our golf skills, the time it is going to take is often overlooked. There is a passage from a book, *First Steps to Golf*, written by G. S. Brown in 1913, that I would like to share with you. "The old proverb that it is necessary for a child to walk before it runs is absolutely true on the links. At the present time one sees thousands of golf children trying to run, when in reality they cannot walk."

Before going to your appointment for instruction, realize it is just that - a session of instruction. **It is not a test.** Some golfers try very hard to make a good impression on their instructor. Please do not be concerned about how you are going to look to your instructor. You are not going to embarrass yourself. Relax and be yourself, and the lesson will go just fine. Remember - it is not a test!

Before getting started with lessons it helps to know that progress often depends on the amount of time on the task. It is the teamwork between you and your instructor that produces the results that both are looking for. Students must also spend time on their own. An instructor can provide information, but skill must come from the student. **Golf is a game of control based on freedom and self-control.** As you start to gain experience, remember this alone will not lead to progress. It is what you do with the information and experiences you have that leads to the progress you are looking for in your game.

There are very few golfers who have a lot of free time to spend working on what an instructor may suggest. So be prepared, and understand that the learning process takes time. Your style or approach to your swing can change and improve, but it will take some time on the task. **I suggest that you practice *what-to-do* with the golf club rather than focusing on trying to fix bad habits.**

Before you make an appointment for your lesson, try to gather some information about the instructor. Some professionals give a large volume of lessons, and this can be an indication of their skill. Find out if this instructor works with a wide range of golfers: men, women, and high and low handicappers. All efficient golf swings are similar through impact but the approach to coaching may vary with each student.

Other golfers might be a good source for obtaining the name of an instructor you could consider. You may see or play with someone whose game you like; ask where they have taken lessons. If you feel the golf staff at the club or course where you play most of your golf, and who see you on a regular basis, are not the ones who can help with your game, ask for suggestions on who you could make an appointment with. Take the time to find an instructor you feel is going to take a real interest in you and your golf game.

The final "Before" suggestion - there is a chance you may feel you are not improving or perhaps even regressing after taking lessons. This is only natural. But if you are aware of this feeling before taking your lessons, you have started to understand the whole lesson experience.

During Instruction

Be early for your lessons. You could use the time while you wait to start your lesson to warm up. But if you are late, everyone's appointment for the day will be off schedule. When first meeting with your instructor, I suggest you tell him or her what you would like to work on during your time together. At times you will suggest one area, only to have the instructor suggest working on a different area first. At times an instructor, when trying to be polite to a member of his or her club, is intimidated and backs off. As the student, not letting this happen ensures that your lesson will be more valuable.

You may want to work on "C" or "D" but your instructor wants to talk about "A" or "B" before going on to "C" or "D." Let the instructor do the coaching. Remember, golf is learned in steps and stages. Ask the instructor to explain the why and the what of his or her suggestions. There are times when we decide to take a lesson and expect the coach will want us to make a big change in our style. Our game is way off, and we feel it is going to take a big change to bring our game around to familiar standards. **Often this is not the case.**

Keep in mind the swing you make for the most part is based on your mind-set and pre-swing elements Grip, Stance, Posture, Alignment, and Balance. So even though your game is way off its normal level, it may only be a small suggestion about fundamentals that will bring your game back. In the case of a new golfer, the required movements of a golf swing that would be considered sound are often *understood and performed* by the student long before a useful grip, stance, balance, and alignment are learned. Both the new and experienced golfer should be prepared to spend some time with pre-swing fundamentals.

I know pre-swing fundamentals are not as interesting to the golfer as the swing itself, and because of this, they may become less important than they should be. These seemingly less important parts (Grip, Stance, Posture, Alignment, and Balance) can be important.

When an instructor asks his students, "What would you like to work on today?" a common answer is, "I can hit my irons but my woods give me trouble." Please realize the basic swing is similar for both woods and irons. After looking at a few swings, my coaching eye will see the same habit with both. The only difference is that with the shorter irons the habit is smaller than with the longer woods or clubs. Students are misled by the iron shot that is only 5 yards left or right and still hits the green, not realizing that the same swing with the wood would produce a shot that is 15 or 20 yards off line. So, "Let's work on the woods" is the student's suggestion. Do not be unhappy when your instructor wants to work on the fundamentals of golf because then both of you are headed in the right direction.

When making swings during your lesson, it may be helpful to understand that because you cannot see yourself swing, you may be making a swing that is different than the one you think you are making. We can also be misled by what we *feel* when making a swing. **It is important that you and your instructor work together until both of you understand and can *mentally* see the same swing.** If you see some progress during your lesson, this is fine. But do not be disappointed if you do not. The suggestions given in a lesson may take some time for your own style and feel to adjust to.

When working with a new suggestion, it is not useful to say to yourself, "This feels funny or awkward." This is a negative thought. Just say, "Well, this feels new, and I will give myself some time," or "When I have more experience I will do better." Percy Boomer told us "Habit, good or bad, in golf or outside of it needs time to consolidate."

During a lesson, ask questions, and take notes. Get your instructor to give you a few different pictures of what he or she would like you to do. When you have more than one way or picture to make something happen, you will add an element to your game that can only help. The body does not learn, but the mind can.

During a lesson you may hit some very nice shots but feel this will not happen on the course. This is sometimes true, but after more understanding, training, and coaching, you will be able to bring your practice range swing to the golf course. During the lesson, your instructor will probably want to make only one or two suggestions. Do not feel short-changed. We can only practice one part of the swing at a time; more than that and the lesson would be less helpful. At the completion of your lesson, ask any questions you like, and then find out when your instructor would like to see you again.

When working on your golf game do not forget the short game. Pitching, chipping, and putting make up over 64% of the swings we make in a round of golf. Instruction in this area may be more helpful in lowering your score than the long game instruction.

After Instruction

What students do after a lesson will make a difference in the type of progress they enjoy. It is important to have a clear understanding of the suggestions your coach made about your style. But, it is what you do with those suggestions that is going to make a difference in your game.

Let's look at the round of golf with a score of 100. You are on the course for 4 to 4-1/2 hours and take 2 putts per hole. That leaves 64 shots, of which let's say, 14 are chip or short shots, around the green. This would leave 50 full swings. Fifty full swings is a bucket of balls at the range (say twenty minutes to a half hour to hit them). In fact, because each ball takes only a few seconds to put in place and hit, you could say 50 full swings are only a few minutes of actual swing time. You have been on the course for hours, but only minutes of swing time to show for it. Can you imagine practicing typing for minutes each week? Progress would be very slow. So my suggestion to any golfer (whether you are working on a new suggestion or trying to keep your game in shape) is to always have swing time off the course. A few hours of practice time is like playing several rounds of golf.

When playing golf, tips from others are as free as the rain from the sky. Please do not be a willing target for tips from other golfers. Friends mean well, but often they are going to slow the process down. You will only drown in these well-meaning suggestions. (They will not be making suggestions on how to learn.) At the practice range or on the course, your main challenge will be to keep using the suggestions your instructor has given even when you are hitting poor shots. Poor shots are part of the process. It is like misspelling a word. Remember that we learned how to spell by misspelling.

There is a point where golf becomes a self-taught game. An instructor can make us aware of basic core knowledge - but as we start to train and practice, remember that we are teaching ourselves the game. Instructors cannot teach you, but they can help you to learn. I feel this insight is the corner stone of the after-lesson segment of the lesson experience. We can teach ourselves when we train correctly. Keep in mind that you will have good and bad days. Any and all golfers at every level experience ups and downs throughout their golfing history. Understand your golf game will always be hot and cold. Your challenge is to bring the two natural extremes together more often than not.

When on the course playing, do just that - play golf. Do not get involved with swing theory. **Save any ideas for the practice range**; on the course play golf. Ask your instructor for suggestions for taking your game and style to the course.

When on a practice range take your time between swings. Do not hit ball after ball quickly. Take your time with what you and your coach are working on. Always swing to a target, but change clubs and targets frequently. This is a must if your practice is to be useful. **Be playful!**

I feel most golfers fail to reach their potential not because of a lack of talent as golfers, but because of their inability to be an efficient learner. I hope the suggestions made here will help your understanding of the lesson and learning experience. I truly feel most golfers can reach their potential when they improve as students of the game.

You and Your Instructor

See the speaker as having little authority when we are trying to learn. The effective teachers are not trying to convince you of anything. They are not asking you to follow and are not advocating a particular swing. The effective speaker is asking that we observe together with them.

You can think together and observe but not as one mind - *there is a difference between thinking together and having one mind.* Together implies that you and the speaker have a responsibility to look objectively as you share information. It is not that the speaker indicates and then you see, but in thinking together you see it for yourself. If you do not understand in your own consciousness why the speaker thinks what he or she does - the speaker will only bring more confusion.

See the speaker as completely anonymous. The speaker truly is not as important as finding out for yourself if what is being said is relevant for your progress.

Please bear in mind that together you and the speaker are exploring. There is no question of following the speaker. There is no authority invested in him or her. This must be said over and over - as most of us do have the tendency to follow and accept, especially from those whom we think of as a somewhat different, or advanced - and all that nonsense. If you merely follow, you are only following the image that you have created about the speaker or about the symbolic meaning of their words, and progress will not take hold. We are human *beings*, not human followers! Following does not fully engage the high cortex of the brain (where learning is encoded).

One of the factors of intelligence is to uncover and explore. Without personal insights about what is actually going on, we have no measure by which to observe and grow.

Golf - a game to be played, not a subject to be taught.

The information in "You and Your Instructor" is based on notes I made while reading The Flame of Attention, *by Krishnamurti.*

Learning and Improving

Conscious thinking can interfere with simply unconsciously doing; and words can build barriers of misunderstanding. When attention wanders it is not that you have lost concentration so much as you have lost what you were supposed to be concentrating on. You are now attending to something quite different from what you intended.

You have been distracted. But a distraction is merely an attraction elsewhere. A new more compelling thought has emerged from the background and drawn your attention to it.

You cannot be distracted without your own complicity. For example, at first your energy is directed at doing the task; then energy is resisting the effort to do the task; and finally, the energy is directed at fighting the resistance. All this energy and resistance is yours. You have fielded both teams as well as the referee. Exhausting! It is more efficient if, instead of compelling your attention to a task, you allow your attention to be attracted to it.

In tennis, the advice to keep your eye on the ball is forced attention. Find something interesting in the ball is putting a light on the ball that is personal in nature.

Tennis pros who tell their students to notice the patterns the ball seams make, or to look for the brand name as the ball comes to them are suggesting ways of drawing the eye to the ball rather than forcing it there.

The best golfers have evolved techniques for collecting their concentration and centering their energies. **They are using what are now unconscious patterns of addressing the ball, waggling the club, or looking at certain spots a certain number of times.** Everything they do is aimed at keeping themselves free from inappropriate tensions that will interfere with the delicate balance between causing and allowing.

The golf swing is an action in which certain things are caused to happen and certain things are allowed to happen, and faults arise in trying to cause what should be allowed. There is no such thing as an isolated movement; everything is connected to everything else. The smallest movement, the slightest tension, reverberates throughout your body in a spiraling wave. A new balance is constantly sought with compensation here, compensation there. And as the compensations spiral through the body they affect the messages sent by the brain. **It is a whole golf swing, not a list of technical details.**

It is difficult to think in wholes when we have grown up analyzing things into bits and dealing with them separately. What is left out is as important as what is there. **To understand what is meant, one must understand the whole, not each part.** Video replay is probably best when they are short and *without narration.* They are best watched in a receptive mode with soft eyes, not analytical. They are best when the whole is absorbed rather than looking for details. New studies show that they seem to be best when watched after training or even the next day. **Body action should be developed in a way so that the art of the action becomes an unconscious, playful, intuitive whole.**

Progress requires making contact with our fears, anxieties, reactions and habits. Realizing the opponent is not an opponent but rather a partner engaged in helping us understand ourselves more fully is sometimes the first step.

Sharing is efficient instruction. When instruction is in the form of sharing information, not only is it retained, but the instruction also improves. When learning motor skills, actions and movements must be playfully experienced. Verbal descriptions do not give sensations. Words can only give a part of the meaning of movement. Movement must be playfully experienced. Empty your mind so that there is room for new learning. *Forgetting can be an act of learning.* Tiger Woods said, "Too many people get caught up in the last bad shot they hit. I say it is more important to let go of what just happened and let each shot be a new one."[23]

To make progress with any motor skill we must be patient. Without setting a time limit on how long learning will take. Everyone learns at a different rate. We should be in the present, in the now, not in the future or past. When doing something, do it to your fullest, be engaged and in full contact with yourself and your environment, so that your energy is not dissipated and is always available.

In the present there are no regrets. When you are doing what you are doing and nothing else (eliminating following how-to directions), you are then within yourself and with what you are doing. To make progress with golf we must conquer haste! Controlling yourself with

---

23 Earl Woods, *Start Something*, pg 36

little things leads to controlling important things. **In the now, there is no failure, only usable feedback for future use.**

We must know our own limits. Accept your limitations for what they are and capitalize on them. Do not try to do everything perfectly; instead learn to improve what you are capable of. Do not compare yourself to others; improve your own capabilities. You can learn from both your good and poor outcomes. When learning seems to stop, it is only a new plateau from which to grow. Avoid trying to copy expert models or trying to fix poor outcomes.

We must move away from the process occasionally and rest the mind and body. Then come back refreshed and restart. When learning motor skills, you must not over-try. When you seek, you cannot find it. Learn to allow patience and stillness of the mind to take over the anxiety and frantic activity of trying. Learn to see action in slow motion and make your mind and body as one. Feel energy coming from your center of gravity (a point in your midsection) flowing out.

To improve a motor skill, learn to influence your breathing. Fill your entire lungs with air and exhale slowly. This will calm your mind, create confidence and create strength. Go with the flow. Do not work against it. Don't push or hit, go with the flow. You cannot expect to be successful until you use self-control.

To improve a motor skill, learn to let it happen. When you think of showing off, or defeating or winning, your self-consciousness will interfere with the performance and mistakes happen. There must be an absence of feeling that you are trying to do it. It must be allowed to flow and happen. The instant you become conscious of trying for harmony and make an effort to achieve it, that very thought blocks the mind and the flow.

Act unconsciously instead of intellectually. Keep your mind on finding a *way*, and not your destination. Stop trying to be good. We should de-emphasize the power of the intellect and improve our intuitive actions. Free yourself from anger, illusion and false passion. *Play like no one is watching you.*

Learn to make fear a friend. Fear is in the mind. Your mind is like a garden and it will grow anything you plant in it, flowers or weeds. See success and fear becoming friends.

Progress is simply a function of awareness. When we are not aware, we do not learn. Awareness increases the quality of performance and pleasure; and learning improves. Being aware is a right-brain function (i.e., images, feelings, intuition). Awareness is often distracted by left-brain actions (i.e., language, logic, analytical thoughts).

Awareness makes it possible to unconsciously understand. Awareness happens when you allow it to occur, but when your attention leaves the present and the now, awareness is blocked and you no longer see the green, feel the wind, and sense the distance. You now see lakes or bunkers and are concerned with making a score. You are now in the future when past experiences are no longer guiding your actions and thoughts.

Awareness is a mental energy or light that makes our experiences known. It keeps our attention engaged with what we are doing so we can learn and recall the feelings of past actions. **Awareness shines a light; it is not trying to get-it-right!**

The natural process of unconsciously learning directly from a playful experience has been undermined by how-to instruction. The word "education" comes from the Latin word, meaning "to lead out." This indicates that the intelligence already exists within us and needs to be drawn out, which I refer to as "out-struction." The true and primary function of play is to draw out what is already there. The average golfer can recognize the difference between a high handicap swing and a professional swing - but may need some help to interpret what he is seeing.

Seeing – Knowing – Learning

Studies have shown:

(A) 85% of all information stored in the brain was gathered by the eyes.

(B) Patterns of motion are influenced by how the information our eyes gather is interpreted.

(C) Our own personal perception of physical activity is the first step in learning a motor skill.

I could go on, but the importance of the eyes cannot be overlooked when it comes to learning a motor skill. The eyes are the window of the mind. The eyes must do more than look. They must see! Remember Sherlock Holmes "You look, Watson, but you do not observe."

Creating appropriate motor skill actions and reaching one's potential requires eyes that can gather necessary information (not a long list of details). Eyes must be aware, not distracted by fear, unnecessary thoughts and self-talk, doubts or other distractions.

Distracted eyes no longer see and they overlook information. Making putts and hitting greens and fairways all become easier when the eyes stop just looking and start to see. Seeing happens when the mind is engaged with the here and now, the present. When the mind concerns itself with past failure, how difficult the shot is, or on results, our ability to perform or create physical activities is severely impaired. When we are engaged, we are *letting-in*; when we are focusing, we are *seeking* - be engaged!

See fairways, greens, and the hole. There are no deep bunkers, big lakes, or hard putts. Just see the target and play your ball without self-talk or looking for trouble.

The following quotes are from *The Zen of Seeing* by Frederick Franck, a book you should consider adding to your library.

"The way of seeing is a way of knowing."

"For my purpose, the shutter clicks much too fast."

"It is the inexpressible, and the inexpressible is the only thing that is worthwhile seeing."

"It's not what the eye sees, but that which influences the eye and that is the spirit of oneself."

"No longer 'look,' but enter into direct contact."

"In seeing there is no choice."

"The eye does not judge, moralize, criticize, it accepts."

"Seeing is not a thing, but an act."

"Often the nervous eye cannot focus, the hand doesn't obey, it is as if I collided with my actions."

"Just give the eye a little time to overcome its panic, to calm down until the hand dares to trust again, for alien forms do not stay alive very long."

"The Zen of seeing is a journey from half-sleep to full awakening. Suddenly there is the miracle of being really alive with all the senses functioning."

"The eye perceives and a reflex goes from the retina, via what is called the 'mind' to the hand. Then the hand traces that picture."

"Nothing is a mere signal of anything but itself."

"The Zen experience is at the same time a direct seeing into reality. The point where the insight breaks through, a way of awakening the third eye."

"We do a lot of looking, but we see less and less."

"We quickly stick labels on all that is. Labels that stick once and for all."

"It is by labels that we then recognize and no longer really see anything."

"Looking and seeing both start with the sense of perception, but there the similarity ends."

Progress Before Words

How did humans communicate and learn before words and language were developed, or formal organize schooling? By being aware, natural, and spontaneous; by doing, observing, adjusting based on past experiences. In their book, *Seeing with the Mind's Eye*, Doctors Nancy and Mike Samuels told us:

"Pre-civilized man in every part of the world lived his existence in integral connection with his environment. His basic consciousness was visual. He thought, felt, lived visually, for he had no language. Primitive man did not need to be made aware of visualization; it was the only way in which he could relate to the world. But, with the development of language and a written system for recording it, rationalized thought came to dominate visual and sensory information.

"As verbal communication increased and language developed, words came to serve not only to evoke image or experience, it also caused the speaker to establish a distance between himself and his experiences. Language as a whole has become so removed from experience that words no longer readily triggered the sensations of objects to which they referred to."

Language is a tool of perception more than a tool of communication. Trying to make progress with words coming from others can slow down the progress we are capable of. We should take personal responsibility for our own progress. We should learn to be aware and react. We should remember our past personal feelings and trust them. We should stop trying to do it right, or have expectations and timetables. Just playfully do, observe, and adjust - in a safe learning-developing environment.

Eastern philosophies have brought about a growing understanding of the importance of individual responsibility for the development of our own awareness. Awareness is a powerful tool for heightening self-knowledge and changing habits. Man was designed to playfully self-develop and self-evaluate, starting from day one.

"Expectations are the surest road to disappointment, they are the contrast between desire and actuality. Your disappointment lies in the mismatch. Goal fixing is out of the natural rhythm of learning. Collect your expectations and consign them to a bonfire. Do not look for results, just act and the results take care of themselves." (*The Centered Skier,* by D. McCluggage)

"For some reason we do not trust and do not fully use the peripheral vision of our minds. The idea is not to reduce the mind, but to bring into play its spontaneous intelligence by using it without forcing anything." (A. Watts)

"We should learn from our experiences (not someone else's). Our problem is that our power of thought enables us to construct symbols of things apart from the experience of things." (A. Watts)

"In both life and art the cultures of the Far East appreciate nothing more highly than spontaneity. Action without thought, a natural way of action. Eyes see by themselves, ears hear by themselves, and the mouth opens by itself." (A. Watts)

Some Laws of Learning

My approach to instruction improved when I became aware of these five basic laws of learning: **effect, primary, exercise, disuse, and intensity**.

Law of Effects:

We accept and repeat responses that feel pleasant and avoid unpleasant ones. This is one of the reasons golfers resist a new suggestion; it does not feel pleasant at first.

Law of Primacy:

First impressions are vital and often lasting. Not enjoying a lesson is one of the reasons people stop learning.

Law of Exercise:

When information is practiced often enough, there is a good chance that a habit can be established, (but avoid rote drills before a skill is learned).

Law of Disuse:

Use it or lose it. A skill not used is often forgotten. The **BEST** time to review and reinforce information is immediately following a lesson.

Law of Intensity:

Vivid dramatic learning experiences are more likely to be remembered than a dull or routine one. To take advantage of this law, use a variety of learning environments while working on the same concept.

CHAPTER SEVEN
School for Learning Golf Workshops
Handouts

Video Research and Motion Analysis

What follows are quotes from research in the *International Journal of Sports Science and Coaching* (Nov. 3, 2006 issue), discussing the nature of learning, video replay and motion analysis.

> (1) "Given the strong agreement among motor learning experts that there is no such thing as an 'Optimal Movement Pattern,' perhaps these programs (video and motion analysis) should include a *warning that copying other performers can ruin your skills."*

(That's a very strong statement about the nature of learning.)

> (2) "Providing extrinsic feedback often *does not* improve performance. Studies show less extrinsic information is better than more."

(Typically technology creates a long list of exact details and information. But the brain does not encode details - it works best with general, just in the ballpark concepts. Also, studies show that following directions creates the kind of stress that slows learning.)

> (3) "Another issue is whether providing immediate feedback actually achieves an improved performance?

> There is strong evidence that immediate video feedback during instruction has a negative impact in the retention phase of skill learning. This should caution manufacturers from promoting the value of immediate feedback."

(Again, a counter-intuitive, but true insight. Video and other extrinsic feedback is not only less valuable than intrinsic self-discovery, they both can fragment learning.)

More quotes about the manufacturers of technology in *International Journal of Sports Science and Coaching* (Nov. 3, 2006 issue):

(4) "Despite all the development in what is called the *Information Communication Technology*, there has been little consideration given by developers and manufacturers into gaining an in-depth understanding of how athletes perceive and are influenced by video by developers and manufacturers."

(5) "Little is known by the developers of technology for instruction about how much, or when, or what type of feedback is appropriate or even if it can be detrimental."

(6) "When reflecting on questions of use, the developer commented that often the features of the software are put into use as the result of technology becoming available rather than a result of research in what is best for the user." This statement was a real eye-opener.

When I had the honor of receiving two National PGA Awards, 1990 Horton Smith Trophy, and 1991 PGA Teacher of the Year, I was on a journey that I am still on two decades later which was to gain more accurate insights into acts of learning and teaching. At that time I had to go beyond golf industry education opportunities to receive help from leading educators and award-winning scientists to learn more about what constitutes efficient learning and teaching. Today I have a deeper understanding of the nature of learning, and what was clearly missing from my approach to instruction for 20 years. Over the last ten years I have been invited to make presentations about learning and teaching on national TV, in school districts, universities, in workshops throughout the United States, and in many other countries. I was also asked to write a chapter in a book about learning and teaching for the University of Tennessee.

New insights from modern science inspired me to rethink and change the information delivery system that I used for 20 years. In 1990, after I joined insights into efficient golf swings with insights into the nature of learning, individuals started learning faster and retaining information longer.

What to do vs. How to

I have found that golfers who are playfully training with insights into basic core information for what-to-do with a golf club make more progress than golfers who are trying to copy how-to directions for moving their body.

In brain compatible learning environments basic core concepts that are just-in-the ballpark, (not technically perfect details) are used for making progress. Natural actions or responses such as; "Just shoot the ball up," or "Just swing the bat," or "Just swing the weight of the golf club," without following specific details about how to do it, is the suggestion here (based on the science of learning). It's the environment that puts forward the most useful model for what to do. Said another way, it's the environment (not technical details from a perceived expert) that puts forward basic core information. For example: the weather dictates what to wear. In business, what to do is based on the needs of the customer. A doctor does not decide what to do next (how best to use the core information gained in medical school) until the patient is examined. A lawyer does not decide what to do with what they know about the law until they know the details of the case they are working on. **To be fully informed, be aware of the environment; it is the only true catalyst of creative playful learning.**

For golfers, awareness of the conditions of the shot they are about to play (up hill, downhill, into the wind, downwind, left to right, right to left, etc.) is clearly the most useful model for determining what to do with the golf club's head, face, and shaft. This approach is far superior to focusing on technical details of an expert model, or how-to directions for moving the body from a perceived expert. In nature everything works best when it responds efficiently to the environment.

Is Your Delivery System for Sharing Information Growing Your Game of Golf?

True or False:

- You should try to "fix" a poor habit.
- You should try to get it right.
- Praise can be punishment.
- The conscious mind is more valuable than the unconscious mind.
- The most useful actions of parents, employers, coaches, or instructors are ones that make you *feel smart.*
- Focusing on "how to" directions is less useful than becoming aware of "what to do."
- Being taught what a perceived expert believes is the "right way" is less useful than *learning* to develop your own efficient approach.
- A conformity approach to progress is less useful than a random approach.
- Learning facts is less useful than developing function.
- A master of anything was first a master of learning.
- Often learning is making an unconscious shift from belief to a fact.
- Long-term learning is encoded after a lesson, and often during sleep at night.

- When learning anything, both workable and unworkable outcomes have value - with unworkable more useful because you can learn from them.
- The most useful time to use video replay is after a lesson, if at all.
- The safety of the environment and the emotional state of the student are evaluated by the brain's past experiences and taken into consideration first. New learning is encoded in our brain third.
- Learning environments are social environments.
- "Golf" is often missing from golf instruction.
- The golf swing is only 5% to 10% of playing golf.
- The golf club moves the ball.
- Golfers with one arm and golfers with one leg have won tournaments.
- Blind golfers have broken 80.
- Golf is one of the hardest games to learn and play.
- Golf is a game to be played - not a subject to be taught.
- Any approach to learning that wants to be efficient must take the nature of the learning process into consideration first.
- Should a consistent golf swing be the goal?
- The ball flight laws - should be the golf club laws.
- The task of an instructor is to make students less dependent on us.

Philosophy for Playfully Learning Golf

It may be difficult to fully describe someone's philosophy about instruction, but some of my feeling about learning can be found in the following: Whatever I know, or what I am given credit for knowing is not very much when compared to what could be known. To keep investigating, looking for "the yet uncovered," to help people grasp unfamiliar concepts so they can make progress, is my philosophy.

- Whenever you try to help a golf swing you can win or lose - but when you help a golfer you always win. Help golfers become less dependent on their coach.
- The student and their needs are always more important than what the instructor wants. **The aim of effective instruction is to be a practical guide.**
- Information does not produce good learning, any more than paint produces good art.
- Any approach to instruction must take the "Nature of Learning" into consideration, if it is going to be effective.
- Mankind is born playful, and we play to learn, **we don't learn to play**.
- What a golfer hears, understands, and remembers is more useful than what any instructor has to say for improving one's golf I.Q.
- Workable instruction does not try to change poor habits, it changes poor insights, and **develops patterns of access to knowledge**.
- Effective advice is student centered, not teacher centered.
- Many golfers see their poor habits as "riddles" that can't be solved and often look to someone else for answers that only they themselves can answer and solve. Progress in golf is founded on the problem solving skills of the student (seeing options).

- "Teaching is really the art of assisting discovery."
  Mark van Doren
- "Telling has never been teaching, and listening has never been learning." Bob Barkley PGA MP
- A "breakthrough" in learning is a breakout, or breakaway from a past point of view, **opening new learning paths**.
- Unquestioned assumptions can cause poor results that new insights often answer. **It helps any golfer's progress to always see themselves as a learning golfer.**
- Golfers should use insights about the Nature of Learning, not just information about the swing when they want to experience progress.
- The word "teach" does not appear in Webster's definition of education or learn.
- Beyond good health and love, perhaps the "desire to keep learning" is mankind's greatest gift.
- Most golf advice and swing models are based on someone's description of body parts in motion, overlooking the alignment and application of force with the club through impact. **The ball flight laws should be exchanged for the golf club laws.**

Random Thoughts on Playful Learning

Efficient approaches to education see students as lights that are burning bright and these approaches are geared for helping students to help themselves to burn even brighter.

Trying to teach is different from helping someone to learn.

Mankind is designed for success, not for failure. We are all perfect self-learners and perfect self-teachers. We self-learn first, then simultaneously self-teach ourselves to use what we have learned for thriving and surviving.

Encourage the "joy of doing," instead of trying to outdo.

What is it from the past that is getting in the way of future progress?

It's important that the individual who creates the poor outcome, is the one who determines what to do to create acceptable outcomes.

Do not be in such a hurry to get a situation under control that the lesson to be learned gets overlooked.

Going to school or taking a lesson is one thing, becoming educated is another.

Acts of efficient learning are made with the best ingredients on earth; **curiosity**, **imagination**, and **improvisation**.

Following directions or restating facts when learning does not engage personal evaluations, synthesis, reasoning or deduction skills, which stifles motivation and diminishes creativity, turning the joy of learning into drudgery with a negative influence on self-image.

It seems that the main focus of educators, instructors, parents, or employees should be to **make** the individuals they are sharing information with *feel smart* ***and self-reliant***.

Learning is influenced by change and unfortunately many individuals believe making changes requires trying to "get something right," or trying to fix something. Studies show that fixing has never been learning, and trying to "get it right" creates the kind of stress that fragments progress.

It's been said what we do not know can hurt us, but it's what we believe, that is not true, that fragments progress to solve problems.

The brain is a sense making, problem-solving organ. The mind may like calm, but the brain uses chaos.

If students are not changing, then approaches to education should change.

Minds are like parachutes; they only work when they are "open." Many minds have become air balloons, and we know what they are full of.

Ordinary things can produce extraordinary results. (Note: the number 1 and the number 0 are running every computer in the world.)

Try for excellence with what we have, and what we have will improve.

Students accomplish what may seem impossible, if teachers see it as possible.

Workable learning environments are guiding the skills of performance improvements, not looking for perfection.

Efficient approaches to learning ask students what they would like to improve.

Efficient approaches to learning improve a student's capacity to learn.

Students want to learn. Judge them and students will not make the kind of progress they are capable of.

Create self-motivation. Develop a trusting environment.

What we pay attention to grows, what we put aside withers.

It is students who often reveal the best way to help them experience the kind of learning that lasts.

Learning is brain on, hands on entertainment, as students invent their own skills.

Pointing out mistakes is a poor motivator.

It's important to ignore mistakes and redirect behavior elsewhere.

How effectively individuals learn depends on what educators focus on.

The more attention paid to any behavior, the more that behavior will be repeated.

Students must trust their teacher and trust grows and develops when teachers provide non-judgmental environments.

Trust grows by focusing on the positive.

Create trust with the principle of do no harm.

Teachers are always "reinforcing" something and it is what teachers reinforce that grows.

Evaluation Form for Critical, Beneficial, or Questionable Elements

We could say some things are critical, some things are beneficial, and others are of questionable value. For example, heat is critical to cooking, and maybe a new stove would be beneficial, but not critical. Listed below are elements of playing and teaching golf. Cover up my answers in the second column, then Place **C** for critical, **B** for beneficial, or **Q** for questionable value in front of each element based on your point of view.

Environment	Critical
Shot to be played	Critical
Information Delivery Systems	Critical
Timing	Critical
Emotions	Critical
Mind Set	Critical
Creativity	Critical
Improvisational Acts	Critical
Short Game	Critical
Spontaneous Acts	Critical
Ball Location	B - personal choice
Ball Flight	B - personal choice
Grip	B - personal choice
Time on Task	B - personal choice
Posture	B - personal choice
Swing Ideas	B - personal choice
Expectations	Q - can slow progress
Tempo	Q - many kinds work
Alignment	Q - personal choice
Physical Condition	Questionable
Swing Model	Questionable
Consistent Swing	Q - every shot is different

Questions that Can Enhance Higher-Order Thinking and Playful Learning

- *What may happen next?*
- *What did the ball do?*
- *What do you think caused that outcome?*
- *What do you want to do next?*
- *What has been left out?*
- *How many ways can this be used?*
- *How can this be modified?*
- *What is the most important element?*
- *What would you have done?*
- *What did you first notice?*
- *How many ways can this be done?*

"The kind of questions that have the power to enhance and improve what already exists (skills, systems, products) often approach problems from angles that are very different from how they have been dealt with in the past. By coming to a situation from a new point of view, insights that were being overlooked often come to light. The most fertile questions direct the mind to valuable but over looked corners of the universe of possible improvements."[24]

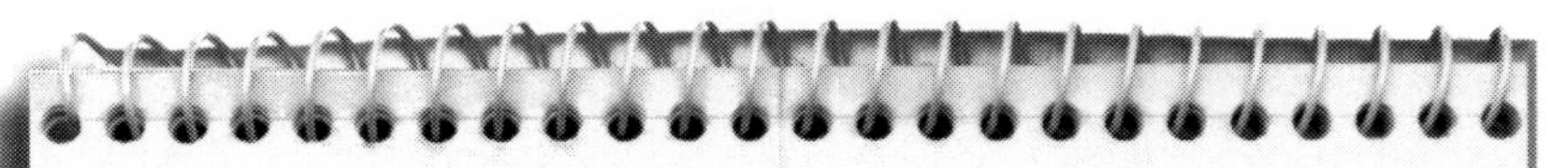

Note: Studies into efficient approaches to learning suggest changing environments every 5 to 10 minutes. For example, when working on alignment aim left for a while, then aim right and then aim straight ahead. When working on tempo, start with one size swing and then move on to another size, and then on to yet another size. The nature of the process of learning suggests that we should avoid spending a lot of time in one context when learning.

24 *Harvard Business Review* (2007, December) pg 73

APPROACH TO LEARNING
Comparison Chart

Michael Hebron's School for Learning Golf

TRADITIONAL TEACHING-FIXING APPROACH	RESEARCH-BASED PLAYFUL LEARNING-DEVELOPING APPROACH
Offer critical observations and judgments of outcomes	Offer positive feedback
Have results as goals	Have process of learning goals
Give directions to follow	Allow students to learn through their own experience
Students are trying to get-it-right	Students are asked to experiment
Students show concern before they act	Students evaluate after they act
Suggest using drills to learn	Uses random experimentation to learn
Teacher has the answer	Individual constructs their own knowledge base
Uses expert models	Uses learning models
Uses out of context aids	Uses in context environments
Uses detailed, specific instructions	Uses just in the ball park, non-specific concepts
Uses how-to directions	Promote imagination, self-discovery, what-if thinking
Teachers are evaluators	Student is the self-evaluator
Uses memorization	Uses indirect preparation
Values current information	Values past experiences
Values following directions	Offers choices

TRADITIONAL TEACHING-FIXING APPROACH	RESEARCH-BASED PLAYFUL LEARNING-DEVELOPING APPROACH
Are result oriented, a get-it-right environment	Are an investment in a students' learning potential
Focus on providing details	Take self-image and emotions into consideration
Try to fix personal habits by focusing on dogma	Focus on the design and structure of the approach to learning
Focus on subject matter	Focus on non-academic skills that support learning potential
Provide answers	Help students create useful questions
Use teachers	Have caretakers of learning skills
Have bias	Have open minds
Use passive learning	Use active learning
Use information from perceived experts	Use interactions by students
Focus on poor outcomes	Focus on poor insights
Attempt to conquer	Use cooperation
Points out failure	All outcomes are feedback
Provides information	Develops a working knowledge from basic core knowledge
Teachers are evaluators	Teachers are sharing
Promotes following	Promotes self-expression
Provides ornamental skill	Focuses on developing useful know how or operational intelligence.
Class sessions are geared for providing information	Develop the capacity for creating knowledge that is personal in nature.

TRADITIONAL TEACHING-FIXING APPROACH	RESEARCH-BASED PLAYFUL LEARNING-DEVELOPING APPROACH
Are judgmental	Provide acceptance
Geared for treatment	Geared for prevention
Uses detailed information	Use reasoning and deduction skills
Try to teach	Coach
Promotes fixing	Develops enlightenment

Tiger Woods Quotes (with comments by Michael Hebron)

"My lie dictates the shot I will play."

"I always listen to my body."

"Some days when I warm up I am hitting the ball low, other days I am hitting it high. Some days the ball is drawing, other days it is fading. I just play what I am doing that day."

> (In 1986, Ben Hogan told me the same story - that he just played what his swing was producing that day.)

"As a junior golfer, when I practiced with my Pop, we always played games trying to make the ball do different things from different situations. High shots, low shots, we tried to make the ball bounce left or right after it hit the ground. We did all sorts of things."

"Today when I practice I still like to play games — in fact I like to practice more than play on the course. I still try lots of different things, just like I did with my Pop."

"We always practiced together seeing who could make the most 5 foot putts."

> (Who could hit it closer to the flag, who could hit the biggest hook, who could hit the highest shot, who could

back the ball up on the range, who could be the most creative.)

"I learned a low 3 wood shot — but at first I was chicken to play it in a tournament."

"It was a **creative-competitive** *environment."*

"On normal shots, I swing 75% of my power, on longer shots I swing at 90%. If I go all out, I do not make solid contact — which is the most important thing."

"As a child, the club and ball became my playmate."

"Ultimately, golf is a journey — full of learning and discovery."

"I love golf — but it must be courted slowly and patiently. Any other strategy will be met with rebuff."

"There are no shortcuts — golf requires patience and perseverance, with a yearning for learning. Accepting the fact that it is a game of ups and downs and learning every time you play."

"I won 12 times in the year 2000, including 3 majors and I only remember hitting one shot I would call perfect. It was a 3 wood on #14 in the third round of the British Open at St. Andrews. As with every shot I attempt, I visualize that ball flight and the shot turned out exactly as I had planned. Moments like that stay fresh in my mind, providing a positive image for future reference."

"When I play — it is almost as if I get out of the way and just let it happen. I let it happen, I do not make it happen."

"I am so in the present that I often do not remember making the swing." (but his subconscious does)

"Often I do not hear any noise or anything when I am playing."

"I will always be respectful and gracious to opponents — but I want to win, to beat you by a lot, to beat you bad."

Success in Classrooms Through Golf

Youth Golf Program Flow-Through Learning©

An Invitation to Succeed
Michael Hebron's School For Learning Golf

One of the aims of our program is to create an interest in learning and playing golf. Said another way, one of the goals here is to make learning and playing golf easier to do than some may believe it can be. At Smithtown Landing there are over 800 young golfers in our program. We believe that golf can be uncomplicated, interesting, and fun to learn and play while enhancing other physical and mental skills.

The program is designed to help students learn "what-to-do," (a positive) and avoids any "How to" directions that try to fix poor outcomes. Studies into the nature of learning show that fixing is a negative approach to progress, and has never supported developmental learning. But by focusing on "what-to-do," long term learning is encoded through the students own reasoning and deduction skills.

Why should children learn to play golf? Some views would say, to win a scholarship; or to develop a great swing; or to win tournaments, or to learn life skills. These views should be rethought and quickly replaced with: **children should learn to play golf simply because it's a great game that's fun to play with friends and family**. Of course playing a game that one loves could result in having that game open other doors. But I have never seen playing a game for the purpose of gaining more from it than the enjoyment the game itself provides open other doors. Scholarships, great golf swings, and life skills may be possible outcomes, but they should not be someone's (parent or child's) reason for playing golf or any game.

There are many skills that the playful acts of learning and playing golf develops unconsciously "flow through" and mix with future acts of learning in other environments, including classrooms. While this may be a counter-intuitive insight, it's a reality. Studies from cognitive science show that past experiences in golf can unconsciously "flow through" and mix with new learning experiences, making them deeper and more meaningful. (I refer to this as "flow-through" learning©, which is a stage of progress that is often overlooked.)

Acts of true play, and what Chuck Hogan calls the "intelligence of play," do indeed improve one's capacity for learning anything. Developmental learning (or what is referred to as real learning) is grounded in the kind of active learning (or play) that enhances one's ability to evaluate and solve problems. When we are learning, making long term progress requires more than the skill of memorizing information. Studies from modern science not only support this view, they suggest that learning golf, more than any other sport, can accomplish this goal. There are several reasons that acts of "play" and "flow-through learning" support progress in schools, and beyond in any real world environment.

Learning and Playing Golf

Acts of Learning and Playing Golf Have an Influence that Goes Beyond Just Developing A Physical Skill.

- Promotes *cooperative* behavior
- Develops *self-control* behavior
- Promotes *reflection*
- Helps develop *locomotors* skills
- Promotes *problem-solving* behavior (critical thinking)
- Aids in *eye-hand* coordination
- Promotes *patience*
- Develops *self-assessment* skills
- Promotes *logical* thinking

- Develops *self-discovery* behavior
- Promotes *self-development*
- Develops *competitive* spirit
- Promotes *sportsmanship*
- Develops cardiovascular *fitness*
- Enhances *emotional-social* growth
- Develops *cognitive* skills (critical thinking)
- Promotes *group interaction*
- Promotes *reasoning and deduction* behavior (critical thinking)
- Promotes *physical* development
- Develops *choice-making* behavior (critical thinking)
- Promotes *pattern and sequence recognition* (critical thinking)
- Helps individual to understand they are *unique*
- Enhances *auditory and visual memory*
- Helps develop *strategy-making* behavior (critical thinking)
- Helps develop both *fine and gross movements*
- Helps develop *alertness and visual-tracking* behavior
- Helps develop *foresight and operative* behavior (critical thinking)
- Promotes combining a variety of *thinking and motor skills* (critical thinking)
- And most importantly, they help to develop *self-reliance* and *self-confidence*
- *Goal-unconscious* (not conscious) thinking and thinking during motor-skill application.

As was said, when learning golf some of the same skills needed to be successful in school and beyond classrooms are being advanced. Golf and "flow-through" learning© improve the self skills: including self-discovery, self-development, self-assessment, self-learning, and self-confidence to name a few. Of all the self skills, self-confidence is the most important when it comes to making progress in life, school and sports. Our program is geared for supporting and enhancing your children's self-confidence and self-reliance.

The youth golf program at Smithtown Landing is designed to help individuals play golf and learn in their own unique way (We do not have to learn to play, we play to learn. Play births developmental learning). **Our program is not trying to teach golf per se, we help students learn to invent their own golf skills based on all of their past experiences.** One of the techniques used to keep a student's interest engaged is to give them choices. Studies show that giving students a choice is perhaps the most meaningful approach for learning and making progress. For example: we may ask, "which way of swinging the club would you choose? showing swings A, B, and C. Our program gives students choices, it does not give commands, criticisms, or judgments of outcomes. Students learn to use their own power of self-assessment.

Efficient approaches to developmental learning are designed to make students feel smart. These approaches take place in smart classrooms and smart learning environments. These environments take into account that **S**tudents' **M**inds **A**re **R**eally **T**errific.

Tiger Woods: "My golf clubs and golf ball were my playmates growing up. From tee to green everyone has a different swing, everyone is an individual, with a different way of playing. I learned the game from the green back to the tee."

More on Self-Reliance

Research into the nature of learning has shown the efficient approaches for making progress are less concerned with changing poor grades and fixing poor habits, than they are about improving learning potential. A master of anything was first a master of learning. To enhance learning potential (not to change poor outcomes) by influencing individuals in positive ways, avoiding negative corrections and judgments, is the focus of our youth programs.

I would think the aim of every parent is that their children become self-reliant, increasing their capacity for learning. This is also the aim of the youth golf program at Smithtown Landing. Our goal is that children discover the joys of playing a game and during the process they enhance their self-confidence and develop a healthy moral compass.

Mark Herrmann's story, "Driving NYU Women's Golf," in the May 10th, 2008 issue of *Newsday* about Theresa Apoznasnski who organized NYU's first women's golf team brought to mind important realities that can be overlooked when it comes to playing youth golf. These realities go far beyond low scores, trophies, and proud parents.

Efficient learning is a process. Learning and playing golf is a process that indirectly develops many skills that flow through and support success in classrooms and beyond in any real world environment. The value of flow through learning is supported by cognitive science, where they refer to it as indirect preparation for more learning. Studies show that learning in one context supports and enhances learning in all other environments.

When Theresa Apoznanski organized the first women's golf team at NYU she was following in the footsteps of two other golfers who also participated in Smithtown Landing youth golf programs. In 1997 Christine Champey started the first women's golf team at Gettysburg College. Christine also helped organize the first girls' golf team on Long Island with coach Tom Kane at Smithtown H.S. In the fall of 2002, Andrea Cody, former captain of Smithtown H.S. girls' golf team, started the first women's golf team at Vassar. Talk about growing the game of golf!

The skills that these young women used to organize the process of starting these first ever golf teams were numerous. They are the kind of skills that go clearly beyond swinging a golf club and a love for playing a game.

Every fall thousands of high school graduates go off to college, why do some have the confidence to organize what did not exist in the past, while other students just follow? Perhaps for these three young women the answer in part lies in the self-reliance and self-discovery skills that were learned while playing and learning golf. These skills (or indirect preparation) supported and flowed through their efforts to organize these new golf teams, which was a process they also learned from.

Playful, non-judgmental learning environments encourage and develop the kind of thinking skills that go beyond the physical skill of swinging a golf club.

Play could stand for **P**owerful **L**earning **A**bout **Y**ourself. These young women were discovering things about themselves and developing other valuable skills in high school in part as they were learning and playing golf. By the way they were playing to learn, and not learning to play.

A young person's ability to evaluate environments and move forward successfully in ever changing real world conditions is unconsciously enhanced when they are learning and playing golf in the ever changing conditions that the game of golf presents.

Theresa Apoznanski, Christine Campey and Andrea Cody are examples (there are many others) of how a positive learning environment can grow self-confidence and helps individuals to invent their own golf and life skills. The higher cortex of the brain, where new learning is encoded is not fully engaged when students are asked to follow directions, or when a perceived expert is pointing out poor outcomes. On the other hand self-assessment and self-discovery fully engage the brain, which is our gateway to learning.

Playing and learning golf has many far-reaching benefits, especially when we play to learn. Theresa Apoznanski, now a pre-med student at

NYU and is one example of what can happen when you are allowed to fall in love with just playing a game that promotes enhancing self-discovery, self-assessment and other life skills.

Over time I have learned that trying to teach golf is less efficient than guiding individuals in the direction of playful self-discovery and self-assessment. When you try to help a golf swing you can win or lose, but when you help a golfer grow their self-skills you always win.

CHAPTER EIGHT
Zen and Playing to Learn Golf

In his books, *The Wisdom of Insecurity* and *The Way of Zen*, Alan W. Watts provided some outstanding insights for making progress. The following is from notes I made while reading these wonderful books that you might consider adding to your library.

When we begin to think about experience, we try to fix it in rigid forms and ideas. We have become accustomed to the idea that wisdom - that is, knowledge, advice, and information - can only be expressed in verbal statements consisting of specific directions. When, in fact, the kind of wisdom which can be put in the form of specific directions amounts to very little, and most of the wisdom which we employ in everyday life never came to us as verbal information.

Yet, these things are performed by the most complex and marvelous processes that no amount of book learning and technical skill can reproduce. This is the real wisdom. **This is the kind of wisdom that we need in solving the real practical problems in golf and life.** It has done wonders for us already, and there is no reason why it should not do more for golf.

Some human beings have ceased to develop the instruments of the body. More and more we are trying to effect an adaptation to life by means of external gadgets. (Teaching aids are often out of context.)

We attempt to solve our problems by conscious thinking rather than through unconscious know-how. Indeed, the special disease of civilized man might be described as a block between his brain (specifically the cortex) and the rest of his body.

Happily, in recent years there have been scientists who have called attention to this block, namely Lancelot Law Whyte and Trigant Burrow. They simply said in medical language that we have allowed intelligent thinking to develop and dominate our lives out of proportion to "instinctual wisdom." As a consequence, we are at war within ourselves - the brain desiring things which the body does not want, and the body desiring things which the brain does not allow; the brain giving directions which the body will not follow, and the body gives impulses which the brain cannot understand.

If a problem can be solved at all, to understand it and to know what to do about it are the same thing. On the other hand, doing something about a problem that you do not understand is like trying to clear away darkness by thrusting it aside with your hands. Many golfers are trying to improve without basic core information that is relevant to golf. Two relevant questions to be answered with a just-in-the-ball-park non technical response are:

What would your swing feel like if it felt good?
What would your swing look like if it looked good?

All questions need a method and a course of action, but we do not need action yet. We need more light. Light here, means awareness, without any judgments or ideas about it. In other words, you have to see and feel what you are experiencing as it is, and not as it is named by someone else. This very simple opening of the eyes brings about the most extraordinary transformation of understanding and shows that many of our baffling problems are pure illusion. **(You already know how hard to hit the putt without consciously thinking about it.)**

The truth is revealed by removing things that stand in the way of its light. This is not unlike a sculpture, where the artist creates, not by building, but by removing. There is no real experience but the present experience. Never at any time are we aware of anything that is not (1) an experience, (2) a thought, or (3) a feeling.

When there is a notion that you are separate from your experience, there will be confusion and turmoil. To understand the moment, you must not try to be divided from it. To understand music, you must listen to it. But so long as you are thinking, "I am listening to this music," you are not listening.

The frightened person begins at once to think, "I'm afraid." This is, of course, an attempt to avoid the experience. **The mystery of life is not a problem to be solved, but a reality to be experienced.** When you playfully experience long putts, or putts with several breaks, you learn how. When there are lots of pre-shot thoughts about results or how hard the shot is, there is little progress.

The truth of Zen cannot be expressed in any form of doctrine. A teacher can do no more than help you get it for yourself.

Zen presents a puzzle to the Western mind because it has taken a restricted view of human knowledge. For us, almost all knowledge is what a Taoist would call conventional knowledge. **We do not feel that we really know anything unless we can represent it in words.** Such knowledge is called conventional because it is a matter of social agreement as to the codes of communication. People speaking the same language have tacit agreements as to what words shall be used for what things.

If we don't miss some golf shots there is no progress.

We can improve by experiencing problems, and being willing to experience problems.

The Chinese written language has a slight advantage over our own. It is linear, but its written signs are a little closer to life than spelled words because they are essentially pictures. As a Chinese proverb puts it, "One showing is worth a hundred sayings." The general tendency of the Western mind is to feel that we do not really understand what we cannot represent and communicate by linear thinking and words.

Seeing and feeling can be paralyzed in yet another way. For when a human being is self-conscious and so self-controlled that he cannot let go of himself, he dithers or wobbles between opposites, and this is precisely what is meant in Zen by going round and round. The mind-body must, of course, trust information in order to act, **for paralysis will soon result from trying to remember whether we have remembered accurately**. But to keep up the supply of information in the memory, the mind-body must continue to playfully act on its own. It must let go of itself both in the sense of trusting its own memory and reflection, and in the sense of acting spontaneously, on its own going into the unknown. In the end, the alternative to a shuddering paralysis is to leap into action regardless of the consequences. **It is necessary for the mind to try to let go of itself and stop trying to be right; trying to fix-it slows down progress.**

Zen is a medicine for all the negative effects of conditioning, for the mental paralysis and anxiety that come from excessive self-consciousness. When practicing Zen it is not true practice so long as we have an end in view. **To practice with an end in view is to have one eye on the practice and the other on the end, which is lack of engagement, lack of sincerity. (Learning is random.)**

Breathing should be without strain, with the focus on the out-breath, and its impulse from the belly rather than the chest. This has the effect of shifting the body's center of gravity to the abdomen so that the whole posture has a sense of firmness, of being part of the ground. Slow, easy breathing from the belly works upon the consciousness like bellows, and gives it a still, bright clarity.

The basic idea of Zen is that it has nothing to say, nothing to teach. Truth is self-evident, so obvious that explaining it conceals it. A non-creative, how-to, following environment is one that bombards us, overloading our switchboard with words. By finding a way of *centering*, the same environment becomes creative again.

As soon as we recognize that a voluntary, purposeful golf swing happens spontaneously (just like breathing, hearing, and feeling), we are no longer caught in the contradiction of trying to be spontaneous. By seeing this, the compulsive and tied-up feeling vanishes. It is just as if you had been absorbed in a tug-of-war between your two hands, and had forgotten that both were yours.

CHAPTER NINE
Recalling Feel vs. Words

Perhaps an initial requirement of making progress is to understand that muscles do not understand words. Muscles receive information from the eyes, our sense of touch, taste and hearing. Be aware and open; develop your own personal language based on your senses. What does it feel like to you? What does it look like to you? Your answers will lead to progress. Remember you are the only one in this world that knows what it feels like for you to putt the ball 15 feet on a slow green. You are the one who has the usable answers, and hopefully the answers are word-*less* - they are in your mind and body and cannot be explained with words. **A picture is worth a thousand words only when no words are used to describe the picture.**

Information to Nowhere

If a golfer was to gather new information about their swing, then think about it on the golf course, in most cases they would be in for a performance below their potential.

How many times have golfers dropped a few balls on a putting green and playfully made a few swings without any thoughts and they all go in? How many times have you made more good shots at the start of your practice when you were just trying to warm up, than in the middle or end of the session when you were thinking about every swing?

We play better golf recalling how a swing feels, than by trying to remember all we know about the swing. Avoid the knowledge to nowhere approach when playing golf. Re-evaluate and review your game when practicing. When playing, be playful, just let it happen. SEE pictures; DO NOT use words; recall feels, DO NOT explain.

Staying In the Process

When students are not pleased with their progress, some start to try harder, and trying harder only slows them down. Do not push the process; trying to get it right will not accelerate learning. **We cannot think about improving; this will only distract us from real learning.** Be free of time frames. When you are not pleased with your progress and feel you are moving along much too slowly, trying harder will not speed up learning. Stay in the process without judgments of outcomes that should be seen as feedback for the next swing, not as failure.

The light will go off when it's ready, not before. Stay aware and past experiences will unconsciously switch the light on. The *greatest* breakthrough any golfer can make is to be unconsciously on par or be synchronized with the enlightenment of past experiences. Keep in mind, mistakes are feedback, not failure, and they can lead to progress if we use them correctly; they are part of the process. Stop trying to do it right, and just do it and accept the results and learn from feedback. **The human race is designed to thrive, develop and succeed, not to fail tests, or miss putts.**

Playing Leads to Progress

When it comes to learning, keep in mind everyone makes progress at different rates. Well meaning friends, some who are accomplished golfers and some who are not, are all going to make suggestions on how to improve your game. They will not be giving you information on learning to make progress. They will be telling you what they think you should be doing, and there is a big difference.

Remember, what is true for them will likely not be true for you. Your strength, coordination, and past experiences may not be the same. Everyone has his own private pathway to progress. Many major breakthroughs for making progress occur unconsciously. Learning is random.

Making progress with golf is mostly playful self-organization, playful self-development and playful self-discovery. Learning is being engaged with the present that unconsciously mixes with the indirect preparation of your past experiences. Playful self-development and self-assessment lead to progress.

"Observe things as they are and don't pay attention to other people."
Huang Po

"Everyone is in the best seat."
John Cage

"All know the way; few actually walk it."
Bodhidharma

"There's only one corner of the universe you can be certain of improving and that's your own self."
Aldous Huxley

"The truth knocks on the door and you say, 'Go away, I'm looking for the truth,' and so it goes away. Puzzled."
Robert Pirsig

"Knowledge is one. Its division into subjects is a concession to human weakness."
Sir Halford John Mackinder

"Once in a while it really hits people that they don't have to experience the world in the way they have been told to."
Alan Keightley

"Believe those who are seeking the truth; doubt those who have found it."
Andre Gide

"Do not seek to follow in the footsteps of the men of old, but do seek what they sought."
Basho

Past Experiences

Golf is a creative process. Artists, actors and sculptors are always learning and growing from past experiences. Golfers should be no different. To make progress with motor skills we must take advantage of our past experiences (both good and bad) and use them as a foundation for future physical activities. Your past feelings will provide the most useful feedback your body can use when learning a motor skill.

When learning a motor skill such as playing golf, each and every swing is a separate performance or creation. A round of golf is not one game, but 80-90 or 100 separate times the brain tells the body what to do. Stay open and aware to what you feel and see when playing. Your ability to make progress when learning golf will be influenced by your ability to use these visualizations and feelings.

"To understand, one must have a very sharp, precise, clear mind; not a cunning mind, but a mind that is capable of looking without any distortion, a mind innocent and vulnerable." Krishnamurti

"Inaction may be the highest form of action." Jerry Brown

Progress

The education of children in Great Britain and the United States has two major philosophies, the "traditional approach" and the "progressive approach." The traditional approach is based on giving children a certain body of information considered essential for their mental development. This information is presented, to use Dewey's term, "from without" in a disciplined and highly structured manner. Subjects are not necessarily related to each other, nor is any emphasis placed on making the material relevant to the student's experiences. The child's task is to absorb the information and to reproduce it in examinations; those unable to do this are labeled failures. The weakness of this approach has become increasingly evident. Some of the information received in a school's "teaching-fixing-to-get-it-right" approach to education is irrelevant.

Making progress requires individuals to be able to think for themselves and to adapt to different circumstances (to develop know-how or "operational intelligence," a Piaget term[25]). The progressive philosophy of playing-to-learn is based on the principal of education from within. It sees the task of learning as the creation of free, direct, playful experiences whenever possible. Emphasis is placed on the process of learning rather than on the subject or results. Play-to-learn approach develops adaptability and creativity on the part of the student. Freedom from restraint and rigid structures is only the beginning. The playing-to-learn training finds a way of developing the inner freedom that is an essential part of progress that lasts. The goal is spontaneous, improvisational thinking, and flexible and portable skills.

"To reach perfection, we must all pass, one by one, through the death of self-effacement." Dag Hammarskjöld

"When you're green, you're growing. When you're ripe you rot."
Ray Kroc

25 Jean Piaget, *The Theory of Cognitive Development*, one of the most historically influential theories in the field of development psychology.

CHAPTER TEN
The Joy of the Journey

To make progress when playing golf enjoy the time on task it requires. It must be interesting and fun for you to practice. If you are playing golf to please someone else or for what you may someday win or receive, it will be very difficult to improve to the level that you are capable of. Simply put, we must enjoy the road to progress. The journey must be at least as enjoyable as - if not more enjoyable than - reaching the destination.

"Blessed is he who has found his work. Let him ask no other blessedness."
Thomas Carlyle

"If the building of a bridge does not enrich the awareness of those who work on it, then that bridge ought not to be built."
Frantz Fanon

"Enjoyment is not a goal, it is a feeling that accompanies important ongoing activity."
Paul Goodman

Absorb

When you let the body react to information the brain absorbs and receives from the target, you are permitting the creative process to influence learning. When we react, we are more accurate than when we think. When relying on conscious thoughts, the body does not understand this language and receives inaccurate and useless information.

The information that is needed is always there, you don't have to look for it, just take and absorb what is. You can feel the wind, see the hills, and sense the texture of the sand. Just let your brain gather the information and permit your body to react without thinking or telling yourself what to do with words, see and feel the shot at hand.

"Mountains should be climbed with as little effort as possible and without desire. You climb the mountain in equilibrium between restlessness and exhaustion. Then, when you're no longer thinking ahead, each footstep isn't just a means to an end but a unique event in itself." Robert Pirsig

"You're involved in the action and vaguely aware of it. I'd liken it to a sense of reverie — it is not merely mechanical, it is not only spiritual; it is something of both, on a different plane and a more remote one." Arnold Palmer

"When I play my best golf, I feel as if I'm in a fog. . . standing back watching the earth in orbit with a golf club in your hands."
Mickey Wright

"I wasn't worried about a perfect game going into the ninth. It was like a dream. I was going on like I was in a daze. I never thought about it the whole time. If I'd thought about it I wouldn't have thrown a perfect game — I know I wouldn't." Catfish Hunter

"The body moves naturally, automatically, unconsciously, without any personal intervention. But if we begin to use our faculty or reasoning, our actions become slow and hesitant."
Taisen Deshimaru

"More wisdom is latent in things-as-they-are than in all the words men use." Saint-Exupery

"Golf is an exercise in perception: every shot requires that you estimate where you are in relation to the target."
Shivas Irons

Don't Think

Seeing and Change

There are no shortcuts when developing a motor skill. It takes a mind that is open and eyes that really see. See where your skills really are. Don't fool yourself. When you have a true picture of your skills, you now have a realistic understanding of what you can expect. With unrealistic images of your game in place, your golf will stay stagnant. Progress will not occur unless you are open and aware. Be prepared to make changes when learning golf. You may have to see things in a different way before you can experience progress. Changes can make you uncomfortable. Any change you have introduced can take you out of your comfort zone.

Try not to use expressions like "this feels so bad" or "this feels strange" when you make a change. The brain will not accept change if it is being described negatively. Just say, "this feels new" and stay with it until it becomes more familiar or comfortable. Remember to stay open, aware, and take your time when learning a motor skill.

"What is moveable is always superior over that which is immovable. This is the principle of controlling things by going along with them, of mastery through adaptation."
Lao Tzu

"Keep your hands open, and all the sands of the desert can pass through them. Close them, and all you can feel is a bit of grit."
Taisen Deshimaru

"How is it that little children are so intelligent and men so stupid? It must be education that does it."
Alexandre Dumas

"Flow with whatever may happen and let your mind be free: stay centered by accepting whatever you are doing. This is the ultimate."
Chuang Tzu

"When we pay attention, whatever we are doing — whether it be cooking, cleaning or making love — is transformed and becomes part of our spiritual path. We begin to notice details and textures that we never noticed before; everyday life becomes clearer, sharper, and at the same time more spacious."
Rick Fields

"We do not err because truth is difficult to see. It is visible at a glance. We err because this is more comfortable."
Alexander Solzhenitsyn

Try not to use expressions like "this feels so bad" or "this feels strange" when you make a change. The brain will not accept change if it is being described negatively. Just say, "This feels new" and stay with it until it becomes more familiar or comfortable. Remember to stay open, aware, and stay playful when learning a motor skill.

Behavior and Progress

We live and behave according to our past experiences. Thinking is a process born out of experiences stored in the brain as memory. From memory there are unconscious thoughts and actions. From action there can be new learning and a cycle of progress. We cannot truly observe if our mind is preoccupied and to observe there must be the freedom to observe.

The word *discipline* comes from the word *disciple*, and an efficient disciplined mind is learning from its own observations, actions, and heart, and not from a teacher or books. Making progress through observation requires a certain discipline, but not conformity.

When there is conformity, obedience, and copying, there is little progress or learning, only following. Discipline implies progress and learning from our daily existence with a mind that is always pliable. We are entirely responsible for our own actions and making progress from them. **When we live for conforming, obeying, copying, and repeating, we lose our capacity to learn from our own actions.** We are human *beings*, not human *followers*. We learn by *being*.

We should understand the difference between concentration and attention. Concentration implies bringing all your energy to a certain point, whereas attention is open and has no control. When we are playfully attending, the brain does not try to record; rather, it's free, utterly still, observing, and letting-in. Focus and concentration are not as useful as attention and engagement.

Problems Are Opportunities

What is a problem? Is it something we have to face? How does one approach a problem? **The way you approach a problem is more important than the problem itself.** Generally problems are approached with some fear, to go beyond them, to fight them, to escape from them, to neglect them, or maybe to put up with them.

How do you approach a problem? What is your motive? Motives dictate one's approach. If we approach a problem freely and openly, without a motive, we can come very close to it. **We see the answer in the problem and will not look away for the answer.** When playing golf the answer is in the shot that is about to play - not in someone else's how-to directions. When we approach a problem with a motive, the problem and our solution will be distorted.

When the mind is free of technical details and how-to directions you can recall the feel of both your good and bad swings; you can pay attention to what your swing feels like - and progress is on the way. When trying to improve one's golf game - if there is a motive beyond progress (if "I have to learn because..."), there will be little progress.

It is very useful to be aware of one's mind-set when approaching a problem. Problems that are not understood become distorted, but when we approach problems without a motive, we are at full awareness and see the answers that lie within the problems. Problems are opportunities!

Are they solely optical experiences, when, for example, you look at a tree and observe the form, pattern, and the light on the leaf? Or do you use words as you walk by - "That's an oak." By naming and using words you are no longer seeing the tree. Can you look without using words? *Just look and putt without thinking words.*

Are you aware of how you approach, look and perceive?

Do you observe partially, with only one sense, or do you see it, hear it, smell it, feel it, and take in the whole of it?

FEAR (False Evidence Appearing Real)

How you approach fear and perceive the whole content of fear influences progress.

Do you see it as something outside of yourself, as though there was a division between you and the fear? Or do you perceive the fear with the whole content of your being so there is no division of yourself - you and the fear are one? Wherever there is division there is conflict.

When we approach fear (which is a mind-set) as though it is something different from ourselves, conflict and struggles come into play. The nature of fear and not the object of fear, how does it arise? Most of us are afraid of something (or of many things) - but we are not talking about what we fear, but the fear itself. Do we fear the putt, or do we fear missing it? If there is motive to go beyond it, suppress it, avoid it, neglect it, we will not see the fear clearly and cannot come near it.

So what is fear? Fear is remembering pain or punishment from the past that has been recorded in the brain. Fear is part of our self. It is not on the outside waiting to be attacked, avoided or handled. Fear is not in the present, it is in the subconscious mind. It is built on the past and looks into the future. See the truth of fear in yourself; it is remembering and approaching the idea of fear with a motive that has divided the fear and you.

There are two ways of negating fear, either by totally denying it, saying, "I have no fear," or by seeing that fear and you are one. This requires no action beyond staying in the present where there are no memories of the past and no looking into the future. In the here and now of play there is no fear.

When we say the putt is difficult, we no longer see or feel it. It is a hard shot only if you think it is. Play one shot at a time; do not drift into the past or look into the future.

When we realize that fear has arrived and it is created and it *is* ourselves, we do not have to get over it, run away from it, destroy it, comfort ourselves against it, or act upon it. There is the non-action of staying in the present where there is no fear.

Another reason for fear is comparison, which is comparing ourselves with others, or with what we have done, or what we would like to be.

Time can be one of the factors of fear - time as in yesterday and tomorrow. The past and the future are not what-is. What-is has no time. It is the present and can be observed without conflict. To understand *what* requires complete observation in the present.

The fear that comes from comparison, desire and time will create a conflict with *what-is* (or the present), causing the mind to be confused, distorted, and therefore, to have no clarity. When we see fear and ourselves as one, not separate and divided, conflict no longer exists, and we can stay (in the present) where there is no fear.

Stress

Stress can be a major cause of a lack of progress. Said another way, trying to follow someone's how-to directions, or trying to fix a poor outcome, or trying to get something just right, can produce the kind of stress that fragments progress. *We can think about doing something, or we can just do it.* It seems that we cannot do both at the same time.

Dr. Robert Sapolsky, Ph.D. (Stanford University) said, "The brain remembers in two ways, facts and procedures. Memories of procedures are damaged if we are trying to recall facts (how-to directions or corrections) at the same time." When performing, just perform; do not try to fix anything. "Tiger Woods faces shortcomings without negative self-judgments. Instead he implements a proactive plan and sees the 'issues' at hand not as negative but as opportunities for self-improvement."[26]

A benefit of truly playing is that there is no stress, unless play is being judged, corrected, or criticized. During true play we first *do*, then *observe* the outcome, and make unconscious adjustments if needed. **Any adjustments are based on the indirect preparation of past experiences, which are at the core of a transfer of learning.** For

26 Brad Kearns, *How Tiger Does It*, pg 93

example, anyone who shoots a basketball for several minutes will not make all his or her shots. When they miss the shot they don't give themselves a talking to about angles and shapes that they must correct. They just playfully shoot up again; any adjustments made were unconscious (a little higher or lower, a little more to the left or right) based on past experiences. They are clearly playing-to-learn and making progress. Golfers should do the same!

Variety is not only the spice of life; it is at the heart of long-term learning. When playing-to-learn both similar and dissimilar past experience to what we are doing in the present unconsciously guide us in the direction of reaching our optimal potential. **The great majority of successful athletic performers have multi-sports backgrounds to draw on.** This insight also holds true in the business world for individuals who have experienced a variety of ever-changing environments to draw on. Constant or consistent environments can become poor learning environments. They do not support a transfer of learning from the indirect preparation that past experiences can offer. In play-to-learn environments both workable and unworkable outcomes are of equal value. In every way, poor results are usable feedback for future reference. **The unforced wisdom found in past experiences honors human creativity, which pilots our ability to adapt.**

The areas of our brain that guide our interactions with the environment are making predictions before we act. These predictions are based on the indirect preparation that past experiences have provided. Information encoded during playful self-discovery has been found to be more useful for making predictions than trying to follow how-to directions from a perceived expert, or copying an expert model, or doing drills before a skill is learned. **A free, unrestricted, playful approach to progress; with just basic core information about the environment in mind, is a brain compatible approach to progress.** For example, a basketball net is up, which is basic core information, and the only reason we shoot basketballs up. Young and old, professional and non-professional basketball players can all shoot the ball up and make a shot. When they shoot, they each have a different style, but everyone is keeping the game's basic core information in mind. (The Basket Is UP.) These players are not engaged with a list of details or technical information. Golfers with a brain-compatible approach to progress have a short list of basic core information in their subconscious mind and are not focusing on technical details.

Mind-Sets for Progress

You will not see progress until you believe you can. When practicing, we are training to make progress. When playing, we should trust what we have playfully practiced. To reach our potential in golf, the differences in playing (trusting) and learning (training) must be recognized and understood. Both require different Mind-Sets. **Golfers who make progress have developed a system of blending, learning and trusting.** When practicing, have a Learning-Training Mind-Set - on the golf course, have a Playing-Trusting Mind-Set.

CHAPTER ELEVEN
Alexander on Habits, Balance, and Playing to Learn

Through Frederick Alexander's research, professional actors and actresses developed techniques to improve their abilities to perform. Frederick Alexander was born in Australia in 1869. More than 80 years after Alexander first presented his insights into making progress, changing habits and balance; people began to realize that he uncovered a powerful tool for playfully changing habits and heightening self-knowledge. This technique that provides useful information for improving any physical activity is known today as the Alexander Technique. Dr. Frank Jones (Tufts University) described the Alexander Technique as "a means for changing response patterns of movement, and improving reflex response patterns."

As Alexander set out to improve on his abilities to perform - or "Use of Self," as he called it (Jean Piaget called it "operational intelligence") - he made several important discoveries. These discoveries would become the foundations of his technique. **Alexander found that tension was the main cause of the misuse of self or of bad habits.** He went on to discover when the misuse of self is allowed to go on for long periods of time, bad habits start to feel natural and correct and become very difficult to replace. The reason Alexander did not discover or correct his "misuse of self" in its early stages was that his brain (and its feel for balance and correct use of self) was not capable of receiving realizable information from the control center of the body, his spinal cord. The out of balance position of Alexander's head during his performance resulted in some muscle spindles going silent and failing to give appropriate feedback information for the brain to monitor muscle contractions and the feel of movement.

Alexander then discovered that when he was not pleased with his performance, he would try harder and harder to get it right, and would create more problems. The pattern of misuse of self was becoming clear to Alexander. **Tension causes misuse; misuse causes bad habits; bad habits cause students to try hard to get it right.**

Alexander had no formal training in either medicine or education, but he found that the dynamic relationship of the head, neck, and torso was the primary factor in organizing human movement. Two extremely influential men of medicine, both of whom testified to the scientific validity of Alexander's work, were Nobel Prize-winning neuro-physiologist, Sir Charles Sherrington and Professor Raymond Dart, the latter a great anthropologist. They were among Alexander's many influential supporters.

I believe Alexander's ideas and discoveries can improve anyone's ability to make progress in golf. The art of unlearning - or freeing oneself of using poor habits - and a playful ability to perform without tension and the "means whereby" approach to progress can be developed **when the over emphasis on achievement is changed**. The following information about Alexander Technique has come from notes I made when talking to Dr. T. Jackson of Westchester, New York, and reading *Body Learning* by Michael Gelb (a book you may consider adding to your library for fuller understanding of the Alexander Technique).

The dynamic relationship of the head, neck, and torso is the primary factor in organizing human movement. The patterns of tension and poor coordination throughout Alexander's body appeared to be synchronized with the imbalance of his head and neck. Going on to examine their relationship with his mental conceptions of his actions, he began to understand that the patterns of misuse were not simply physical. They involved the whole of his body and mind.

(1) Relationship of the head, neck, and torso is of primary importance in determining his level of functioning and in organizing his reactions into a coordinated whole.

(2) Some positions of the body are obviously better than others for both their practical efficiency and their effect on functioning. These positions are called mechanical advantages.

(3) The head, neck, and torso are linked in an extremely delicate and vulnerable postural relationship. The head, besides housing the brain, eyes, ears, nose, and mouth, is also the focus of the two main balancing mechanisms, the optical and vestibular. (Efficient learning is brain compatible.)

When balancing is maintained in movement, the quality of action changes. Movement becomes lighter and easier, breathing becomes more rhythmic, and internal (proprioceptive) stimuli are perceived at the same time as external (perceptive) stimuli to create an integrated experience of the environment. In other words, you have a better sense of where you are (and sometimes even who you are).

Professor Dart points out that fear, anxiety, fatigue and pain all cause postural deviations from the norm, similar to those seen in a startled person. When one falls into a period of depression, pain or fear, the balance of the head, neck, and torso is actually disturbed. When the difficult period clears, one is often left with a habit of carrying the head in an unbalanced way. Fortunately, we do have a choice in the matter.

If we can develop a feel for the subtleties of balancing our heads, we can then begin to take responsibility for our fighting reflexes. **In other words, as we learn about our balanced state, we increase the possibility that our actions will be fresh responses to the moment rather than predetermined.**

Alexander emphasized the key role that the head and neck play in integrating all parts of the body. The first step towards gaining a practical understanding of this role is to find out exactly where your head balances on your neck. Using the tips of your index fingers, point to the place where you think your head rests on your spine. Most people place their fingers much too low; the balance point is located just behind your ears.

Most of us are unfamiliar with another important area -the hip joints. Bend down and pick something up from the floor, then place your index finger at the point from which you bend your torso. Most people put their finger at the top of the pelvic girdle rather than at the actual hip joint. In fact, the hip joints are much lower than most of us think.

An awareness of the workings of all the joints is useful to good use of the body. Our joints not only make movement possible, they are also centers of our kinesthetic information (feel). The information coming from the joints to the brain can be distorted, leading to further misuse. The simple fact is that the majority of us may not know where any of the major joints of the body are located, and we misuse ourselves accordingly. Practical knowledge of basic anatomy and body mechanics will help you in making more accurate observations about what you do with yourself and will give you clues about what not to do.

When observing the behavior of infants, their mistakes (feedback) become part of their experience. They are totally undaunted by mistakes, feeling no disgrace or embarrassment, but rather a renewed desire to explore; thus demonstrating a style-of-life. This desire to do and an ability to learn is what we might refer to as *genius* in an older person.

Realizing the limitations of traditional academic study, Alexander then began to seek guidance from sources based on experience and methods for developing self-observation and self-knowledge. *The nature of the learning process was of fundamental importance in his quest to overcome the dominance of habit.*

Fear is one of the biggest blocks to progress. It psychologically interferes with an individual's ability to respond freely and to function naturally, abilities essential to learning. To make one's fears more accessible to consciousness is the first step to resolving them and to stopping them from stifling the ability to learn. **Fear is False Evidence Appearing Real** (an acrostic for fear).

The field of attention is always reflected in the state of one's muscle tone and balance. There is no way of forcing results. Pay more attention to the "what" of things as a fundamental aspect of one's progress. It doesn't matter if you are right or wrong. It is all useful feedback.

"Surely, if it is possible for feel to become untrustworthy as a means of direction," Alexander wrote, "it should also be possible to make feel trustworthy again." Alexander realized that he must spend time practicing this conscious mode of new direction and that his practice would feel wrong according to his old sensory standard. (A huge insight!)

In order to allow his new reasoned direction to dominate habit, **Alexander concluded that he must give up all thought of the results to which he was working and focus instead on the steps leading to that end (the means whereby).** Alexander worked out a plan. First, he would inhibit his immediate response, thereby stopping at its source the habitual uncoordinated direction. Second, he would think about *what to do* for his improved use of himself, not *how-to* do it. Third, he would continue to project these directions until he was confident.

By staying aware of his actions, Alexander began to free himself from his unreasoned control of his organism. He outwitted his instinctive habitual direction and in the process developed a new method of progress based on the integrity of the psychophysical person. Aldous Huxley said, "If you teach an individual (I would phrase that as help them to learn) first to be aware of his physical organism and then to use it, you can often change his tendencies."

Our reaction to disturbing events throws our bodies into chronic imbalance. Research shows we tend to hold the memory of a traumatic experience in a particular part of the body. This memory in time becomes part of the total pattern and is incorporated into an individual's use of himself (consciously recalling past missed shots for example).

Non-Doing

Learn about non-doing. At first this is baffling, but Alexander went on to discover that the solution to many seemingly difficult tasks is not to try harder, but to leave oneself alone. His organism became capable of much more than he had ever imagined it could be - so long as he did not get in the way.

Alexander learned that if he didn't think or try hard to be right, he could begin to make progress. Alexander was in a vicious circle; habitual response and he would tense up further, and so on. Obviously he had to stop this at its source. He had to inhibit his habitual response and put his attention on the means - whereby the process happened. **He focused on what-to-do, not how-to-fix things, while keeping the general directions for the best use of self in background awareness.**

When Alexander managed to avoid his habitual interference and venture into the unknown, he would learn; Alexander was able to get a better feel. Although his habit patterns were still present, their influence had diminished (bad habits can be sign posts for good habits). In the past he had always tried to get it right by going directly for the end. **Now Alexander paid more attention to the process.** His ability to monitor his performance was also increasing. He seemed to be more centered - more engaged, **letting-in rather than seeking**.

His work with the Technique simply provided an approach for getting more out of his practice and improving his coordination. *He suggested that students playfully journey into the unknown, and pay attention to the means whereby, directing attention to the feel of and the amount of energy used.*

The Technique presents a formidable challenge to those of us who are used to trying to get results by following how-to directions and trying harder. One must find the delicate balance between ends and means, control and spontaneity, doing and non-doing. This problem of balance is expressed in the paradox, **"give up trying too hard, but never give up."**

Alexander said, "You should learn with as little effort as possible." If the pupil makes any unnecessary tensional adjustments, I ask him to note it, and we start over again. The pupil should be exploring and inventing in an unconscious sensory territory. Eventually he realizes that he can playfully learn with much less energy than he had thought. Children are relatively free from fixed habits and have less to unlearn.

The Alexander technique is not concerned with undoing, but with doing. There are no secret exercises. New sensory experiences cannot be gained through written or spoken words.

Alexander felt that any attempt to develop new use, to get-it-right by direct action, was doomed to failure; the process approach must be combined with an attitude of playful openness to the unknown and a willingness to suspend the judgments conveyed by feelings. It is possible to begin to increase your self-awareness and to deepen your understanding of the use of the self by practicing the art of observation. It helps to have objective points of reference in order to get a clearer sense of how we use ourselves; one of these is a mirror.

In order to make effective use of the mirror, or any other form of feedback, we have to learn to avoid making value judgments. **The habit of labeling everything as good or bad, right or wrong, attractive or unattractive is associated with a deep pattern of tension and misuse.** We can begin to free ourselves from this pattern by simply looking at and accepting what is; this is the first step towards real change. *Integration results not from the specific, or direct actions, but rather from an indirect approach, which at all times considers the balance of the whole.* There is no right or wrong way, only what is!

Observing others can provide a valuable source of information for your study. If you can observe without criticizing, you can learn a great deal. Try to get a sense of the distribution of tension, noting which parts of their bodies are stiff and which collapsed. Look at people whom you consider to be examples of grace and poise: perhaps a favorite entertainer or sportsman. Notice what they do as well as what they do not do with themselves (without judging), observing them in a general - not a specific picture.

The biggest problem to overcome in making progress is the fear of unfamiliar territory. Some students start with the idea that they can't learn; they may think they are too uncoordinated or too old. Those who have a more positive outlook can try so hard that they don't really give themselves a chance. **All of them want to get-it-right from the very beginning.** Except for a few extraordinary individuals, this is simply not possible. Attention to a playful means whereby, seems to short-circuit these fears, and it also gets results. Keep in mind, learning is random.

One of the biggest obstacles to progress is preconceptions people have. When students are made aware, they are often amazed to find that they weren't doing what they thought they were doing. Athletes are trained to pause just before they go into action. This allows them to clarify their mental conception of what they are about to do, and to translate that conception fully into the body. Alexander found that most people were unable to direct their attention to themselves, and as a result suffered from mind-wandering or over-fixated-concentration. Attention can become something we give rather than something we have to get. **Attention is letting-in, focus is seeking progress.**

Alexander's aim was to find a new method of dealing with the problems of habit and change. The procedure that Alexander discovered emphasized the process and journey of attaining, but not the goal itself. He discovered that most of us let our immediate goals dominate the field of our attention. Alexander called his method of change the "means-whereby" approach, not goal seeking.

A man who does not stand properly forms a habit of standing improperly, a positive habit. But the outcome is negative. He is failing to do a workable thing, **and the idea that failure can be made good by an order of the will is absurd.** Conditions have been formed for producing a bad result, and the bad result will occur as long as the bad conditions exist.

We must stop even thinking of standing up straight. *Trying-to* (retrieving or forecasting) is fatal, for it commits us to the operation of an established habit of standing wrong. We must find an act within our power that is disconnected from any thought about standing. We must start to do other things which on one side inhibit our falling into the customary bad position (inhibition), and on the other side is the beginning of a series of acts which may lead to a workable posture (direction). Until one takes intermediate acts of the process of learning seriously enough to treat them as ends, one wastes one's time in any effort to learn new habits. In all that concerns life, it is only through the ***indirect*** approach that the most substantial goods are achieved. Learning is based on ***indirect preparation***.

Eugene Herrigel was a German professor who studied under a Zen master for six years. Herrigel's training involved learning archery and he described how each step in the process of learning to shoot became an end in itself. In Herrigel's book, *Zen in the Art of Archery*, he describes the proper inner state. "Stop thinking about the shot," the master would say, "That way is bound to fail."

Just as there are laws of physics that govern the behavior of objects, so Alexander believed that there were laws of human reaction that govern the experience of playfully making progress.

Quotes for Learning

"You can teach a student a lesson for that day but if you can teach him to learn by creative curiosity, he will continue the learning process as long as he lives."
C. P. Bedford

"Clothe an idea in words and it loses its freedom." *E. Friedell*

"Success is a journey, not a destination." *B. Sweethand*

"You cannot hit and think at the same time." *Yogi Berra*

"Millions saw the apple fall, but Newton was the only one to ask why."
B. M. Baruch

"A man paints with his brain and not with his hand." *Michaelangelo*

"When one is painting, one is not thinking." *R. Sanzio*

"Art is ideas. It is not enough to draw, paint and sculpt. An artist should be able to think."
G. Woods

"Good players are good because they've come to wisdom through failure."
W. Saroyan

"Education can train, but cannot create experience."
E. McChesney Sail

"I respect faith, but doubt is what gets you an education."
W. Mizner

"If you see in any given situation only what everybody else can see — you are not so much a representative of your culture — as you are a victim of it."
S. I. Hayakawa

"All knowledge has its origins in our perception."
Leonardo Da Vinci

"A painter who has the feel of it is saved."
A. Renoir

"Hope is a good breakfast, but is an ill supper."
F. Baron

"Hope is not worth the money."
Unknown Author

"The past is but the beginning of a beginning."
H. G. Wells

"Every beginning ends something."
P. Valery

"Communication is saying the right thing at the right time, but keeping quiet most of the time."
N. W. Roper

"The older I grow, the more I listen to people who don't see much."
G. G. Glidden

"Communicating is something so simple and difficult that we can never put it in simple words."
Unknown Author

"Let us train our mind to desire what the situation demands."
Seneca

"The brain is as strong as its weakest think." *E. Dean*

"For the purposes of action nothing is more useful than narrowness of thought, combined with energy of will. *H. F. Amil*

"Think like a man of action, and act like a man of thought." *H. Bergson*

"Do not train boys to learn by force, but lead them by what amuses them, so they may discover the bent of their mind." *Plato*

"Teach the means to education, not things." *R. W. Emerson*

"If the shoe fits, there is no room for growth." *R. N. Coons*

"The purpose of learning is growth, and our mind unlike our bodies can continue growing as we live." *M. Adler*

"There is no failure, except in no longer trying." *E. Hubbard*

"The average Ph. D. thesis is nothing but a transfer of bones from one graveyard to another." *J. F. Dobie*

"Art is the difference between seeing and identifying." *J. M. Norman*

"He who can take advice is sometimes superior to him who can give it." *K. Von Knebel*

"The great end of life is not knowledge but action." *T. H. Huxly*

Learning-Training Mind-Set

It helps to be inquisitive when practicing. Asking yourself or the instructor questions during practice can add understanding and accelerate progress. During a training session, criticizing yourself would be very damaging to your progress. It is not going to help to call yourself names. During training we observe outcomes without criticizing the feedback. We can learn from the past.

Playfully training with a purpose is very important. At the start of your practice session, focus on one portion of your game, not two or three. Always practice to a target and change your club and target frequently. Another suggestion, for every one hour spent on the long game, spend two hours on the short game. Remember, 64% of golf is played inside 60 yards.

Having an inquisitive mind during practice may be fine, but not when you are on the course playing a round of golf. Some golfers have fallen in love with the Practice Mind-Set. Some golfers will overtrain and overlook the enjoyment of playing the game.

Playing-Trusting Mind-Set

On the way to the course, it does not help to fill the mind with expectations, positive or negative. Expectations can be damaging to performance. We should learn to have no pre-set ideas about our golf game when playing. They will only be a distraction. We must stay in the present.

- When playing, the mind-set must be one that accepts what the game is giving on that day. Make swings, and then move on without getting overjoyed or complaining about the results. Accept and move on!

- A "let-it-happen" or "effort-free" mind-set when playing will do more for the quality of someone's game than any other suggestions I could make. When we put effort into our game, we lose control. The mind-set of trying harder is a reason many golfers do not reach their potential on the course. Trying to achieve makes golfers less aware and, therefore, distracting to performing a motor skill.

- Having a quiet mind and passive feelings on the course makes it possible for golfers to reach their potential.
- Please understand **TRUST** will do more for the quality of someone's game than thinking about mechanics on the course. Trust what you have practiced.
- Staying natural or within your own personality when playing is a must.
- Winning is a result - not a cause - of confidence.

TRAINING LEARNING ← BLEND	→ TRUSTING PLAYING
Mind-Set	Mind-Set
Accepting	Accepting
Inquisitive	NO Expectations
Feel of Swing	Quiet Mind
Using Feedback	Let Go! Let it Happen!
Active Mind	Passive Mind; Effortless
Train without a goal in mind.	Trust is More Important than Mechanics
People can fall in love with training and over train, feeling guilty if they miss a session.	Think Target; Be Natural. Trying harder will not let you play your best.

- "Adrenaline," or being nervous, brings you to a higher level; you think better and are stronger.
- We have to be willing to fail - stop trying not to three putt!

- Do not "Pre-Determine" skill level.
- Long-term memory of success, short-term memory of failure (learn to forget).
- Let action just happen (do not think). In golf we have to get out of our own way - no over-thinking. Always think about success; talk about good things.

Paradoxes

- Some things are learned better when we do not try to teach them.
- Some things are learnable, but not teachable.
- Everything we try works.
- We learn more from calamities, than from virtues.
- What is true for children is probably also true for adults.
- Students can learn more from each other than from a teacher.
- Don't try to improve the student, try to improve the situation.
- If you try to fix a golf swing you can win or lose but when you help a golfer you always win.
- We learn to play golf in winter and we learn to ski in summer.
- We should change in the mind (inside) first, and then the physical can improve.
- Changing poor insights changes poor habits.
- **Again, a master of anything was first a master of playful learning.**

Preparing yourself for learning requires an adequate foundation for understanding how the learning and performance of motor skills occur. From this foundation we can then develop appropriate methods for meeting the particular needs of each learning environment.

Knowing the difference between learning and performance is useful. We can unconsciously sense, perceive, attend to, remember, and control movement and information necessary for producing movement.

EXTRA CREDIT

The following contains details that may only interest some readers, but it's information that could be used by every reader.

The Body Already Knows How!

"The Body Already Knows How!" was based on information from notes made while reading John Jerome's Soft Spot In Time *as well as notes from conversations with Dr. Carol Wood, University of Pittsburgh.*

Golfers who are trying to improve may be overlooking what medical, physical therapy, and biomechanical students have learned; the human body knows how to move. It not only knows how to move, but it can also correct inappropriate patterns of motion if our conscious intelligence does not interfere.

We could say that the athlete's job is to learn to do things easily. The highly skilled athlete simply performs in a higher gear, with grace and efficiency. Two elements of athletics are timing and motion, and these require muscle. Muscle works by contraction as it moves the bones of our skeletal system through patterns of movement.

To understand the body's natural capacity for movement (without conscious thoughts); look deep within muscle fiber and membrane where hundreds of strands of protein are laid down in an orderly parallel fashion. It is these strands that contain the capacity for movement.

The signal for movement comes from a motor nerve transmitted to end plates on the muscle fiber. The process starts with the sensory organs receiving information that ignites a burst of activity. A great deal of that sensory information comes, curiously, through the muscles themselves.

One early decision required of the central nervous system is predicting how much muscle will be required to accomplish the task at hand. *Oddly enough, the more automatic (without thought) the response or the further its origin is removed from our conscious control — the more accurate the muscular reaction is likely to be.*
When our dithering minds get involved our muscular reactions tend to become inappropriate. This says more about the slick efficiency of our reflexive system than it does about the interference caused by our conscious intelligence. It is inescapable that our bodies are often smarter than our conscious minds, if we could only learn to trust them.

Proprioception is the sense that tells us where our body parts are in relation to their environment and to each other. Proprioception gives us the capacity (not always fully realized) of smoothly coordinated movement. In close relationship with the organs of balance in the inner ear and with sight, proprioception aids us in keeping bodily equilibrium.

Muscle spindles send signals to the central nervous system rather than receiving signals from it. They help the brain predicted how many motor units to devote to a task. It is this unconscious choice of flexibility that brings fluid grace to human movement. There are also proprioceptors located in the ligaments and the capsules of the joints called joint receptors.

Joint receptors signal to the more conscious levels of the brain than do the muscle spindles. For complex and unusual tasks of coordination, it is the joint receptors that provide most of the information to make the controlled movement possible. For example, the brain must first make a choice to chip or putt.

Finally, there are the Gogli tendon organs located near the junction of muscle and tendon. These are activated by stretch - at very high loading - but they signal the muscle to relax rather than to contract. They are the opposite side of the stretch of movement, inhibiting muscles to prevent injury.

What is important is not so much the control of the body, as is the athlete's ability to unconsciously read the proprioceptive information he is receiving. The sum total of all the firings of all the receptors within the musculoskeletal system unconsciously tell the athlete what his body is doing, or what the relationship of the body parts are and where the parts are headed.

When muscle is contracted or stretched, its temperature rises. As the muscle heats up, it becomes, within limits, stronger and more efficient. Warm muscle fibers simply slide over each other more easily than cold ones. **Furthermore, if the muscle is pre-stretched before contraction, it stores a certain amount of elastic or potential energy.**

The batter in the on-deck circle, swinging a bat before proceeding to the batter's box, may be going through all these motions only because they feel good. They leave him feeling loose, ready. When, in fact, he is pulling muscle group after muscle group toward their optimum stretched length, in effect, waking up the motor nerves, preparing them for the rapid-fire activity that will be required of them to swing the bat through the strike zone with maximum force. He is also raising the temperature of the muscle tissue by all that random flexing, literally getting his juices flowing... He is gaining strength and quickness so he can then put maximum force into his swing without having to over swing in attempting to overpower the ball. *The force can come with a nice, free, easy swing; the kind one sees in the better golfers.*

As a starter's gun goes off for a foot race, that explosion is an event that communicates itself to the brain which in turn communicates an urgent message to a 150 lb. package of meat (or of chemicals and electricity if you prefer). *This is communication of the highest order.* Even the technological immensities of a NASA space shot can't compete. From start to finish, the medium of communication is always electricity. The nerves stimulate the muscles to move the body; the muscles move the bones. At every juncture, at every step on that progression - external stimulus, sensory receptor, spinal cord, cortex, motor neuron, end plate, muscle fiber movement - there is room for improvement!

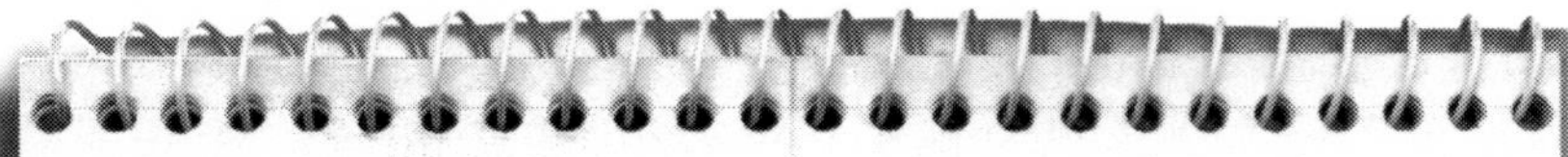

Note : When training skills to playfully turn loose the systems of muscles and nerves responsible for each maneuver, place them on their own, and then stay out of it. In other words, the skill is there, somewhere within the organism. It needs only to be summoned up and turned loose or set to work.

One article of faith in sports is that the athlete seems to pick up a new skill more quickly and with more accuracy than the non-athlete. He or she somehow absorbs the physical requirements of the motor task more easily. But bring a Tiger Woods or a Lorena Ochoa into the laboratory in an attempt to analyze the athlete's ease of accomplishment, breaking down into discrete categories those attributes that permit such quick access to new motor skills, and they disappear on you. *About the only identifiable across the board advantage that good athletes seem to have over the rest of us for reaching their potential is the quality of their attention.* They pay attention to the task at hand a little better than you and I do. Also, they may have more experience at doing other physical activities that require motion, balance, and training.

Perception is always the first requirement for learning to move with skill. But perception is the beginning point for performing a motor task and vision is one beginning point for perception. There are broad-band receptors that respond to the general nature of a stimulus, and narrow-band receptors that pick out specifically applicable stimuli. In fact, sensory information arrives in so many forms, from so many receptors, and the receptors are so closely linked with each other that the individual is a swim in a sea of information.

At the same time that unconscious judgments are being made about all that external information, the athlete must also perceive himself or herself within that environment. Some of these determinations seem self-evident, but many are not.

Research shows that outward movements are seen more accurately than inward movements; short movements tend to be overestimated, longer movements underestimated. Judgments about movements made close to the body are more accurate than judgments about movements made farther from the body. In general, errors in the extent of movement are greater than errors in the direction of movement. Visual phenomena produce less predictable results than do the purely kinesthetic studies. Movement will be spotted more quickly if it occurs near the periphery of your vision than if it is near the center, even though focus is much sharper at the center. An object moving vertically seems to be moving faster than one moving horizontally at the same actual speed. The larger the object is, the slower it will seem to be moving.

An interesting perceptual finding for athletic purposes from a 1960s study which showed that high scores in visual acuity predicted high scores in the faculty of balance, *and balance scores gave the best predictive index to ability in sports.* Nobody is quite willing to say that left-handers make better athletes than right-handers but there is evidence that overwhelming right-hand and right-foot dominance is less prevalent among good athletes than among the general population. "Superior athletic performance is apparently not retarded by left-handedness is the arch way one report puts it. Well-known golf instructor Carl Lohren has been pointing this out for years.

Motivation is critical to individual motor performance. For example, we are capable of doing much more physically than we usually manage, and higher motivation can help make up the difference.

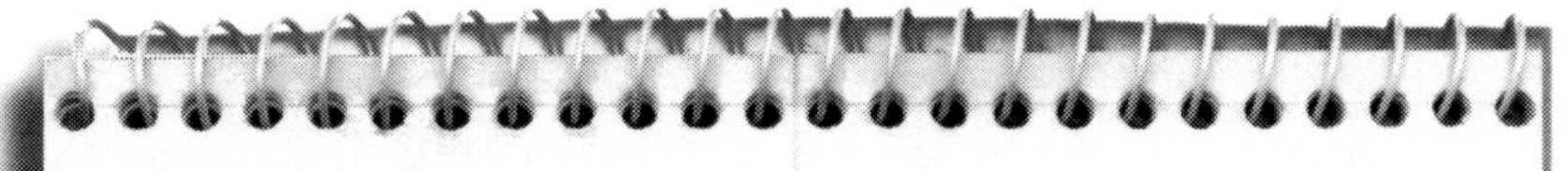

Note: You get better results if you suggest that the subject relax than if you suggest that the subject be more accurate, bear down harder, be steadier.

There is an optimum level of arousal that tends to shade into tension. In preparation for motor performance, tension can be helpful, but too much tension can be a sign of anxiety, which reduces motor performance. Quick learners are more highly motivated and very likely have a lower level or residual tension that might interfere with learning. Playing to learn environments have lower level of stress than teaching-fixing to get-it-right environments.

The ability to make progress varies with the amount of attention the subject is able to bring to bear on the process, but once a particular motor skill is learned, the subject can perform it in the face of rather startling amounts of distraction. ***Some studies show that long practice sessions with very high numbers of repetitions may actually reduce retention.***

With equipment that measures the electrical action potential of muscle groups, researchers have found that *when subjects mentally rehearse a motor task they also fire the correct muscle groups in the correct order,* even if they are actually motionless. One study indicates this mental practice also is more effective in the early stages of acquiring a skill than it is later when the skill is assimilated. The more complex the task is, the more improvement is likely to result from mental practice. Recent studies point to how mental practice is recorded in what is referred to as memory cells in the brain, that fire when we are doing both mental and physical practice.

Once we learn a motor skill, we retain it better than we do other kinds of learning. "It'll come back to you." As motor skills are learned, they seem to require less and less conscious thought - indeed, as Lewis Thomas points out, *"Conscious thought can become a hindrance to their performance."*

Knowledge of Results and Feedback

One of the important roles in making progress with a motor skill involves the results of a particular practice trial. This information, referred to as **Knowledge of Results or KR**, appears as one of the functions that a motor skills instructor performs for the learner. **KR is information about a response that is obtainable by means of an external source.**

"Feedback" refers to data available to the person by means of his own sensory system. KR from teachers, on the other hand, differs from feedback in that it represents information about a response which the person could not detect without the aid of an external source.

After hitting a golf ball, the person can see the results of his or her swing; that is, where the ball went. That person is also able to detect what the swing felt like. Thus, they are able, on the basis of visual and proprioceptive feedback systems, to determine certain aspects of the results of their efforts. However, the person may not be able to detect that they did not take the backswing back far enough, or that the hands were too far behind when hitting the ball. The golf instructor helps the student gain that information. It is this type of response that is labeled KR. **KR is a learning variable that the teacher or coach can directly manipulate and thereby greatly influence learning.** Studies have found that feedback leads to learning that lasts and KR often does not last.

Adams (1971) stated that learning a motor skill is best viewed as a problem to be solved. Accordingly, there is a need to establish what is essential or necessary for this problem solving to succeed. Information about a response in the motor skill situation is important. It will help the student make some necessary adjustments before attempting the skill again. The brain learns best by **doing**, **observing**, and **adjusting**, based on past experiences, not by following how-to directions.

As an example, suppose you have never had a golf club in your hand before and you are beginning golf lessons. As you first begin to learn the golf swing, you may find that you do not clearly understand what the swing is supposed to look like and how it should feel. You have some idea from watching your instructor, but you are not quite sure what your own swing looks and feels like as compared to what it should be. This is where KR as information plays a role. Your instructor may show you things after several swings. In this way, learning the golf swing is seen as developing changes in what you were doing, then swinging again to incorporate the change. Theoretically, the golfer is using KR as information to form hypotheses and strategies about his or her performance, testing the effectiveness of those hypotheses and strategies in each succeeding practice attempt using feedback.

KR can contribute to a learning situation by providing a source of motivation for the student. Motivation is defined as "anything which impels a person to start or keeps the person moving toward a goal." In the example of learning the golf swing, it should be apparent that there is a definite motivational factor involved in continuing to train the skill enough to learn it. Significantly, KR has been shown to have a definite influence in this regard, **but personal feedback is more valuable.**

The important point to appreciate in each of these situations is that it is the instructor or coach who is responsible for providing the response information we have labeled KR, and that is why it is not as valuable as feedback that is personal in nature.

Some KR is necessary for learning to occur, but performance can be maintained without KR. In golf, when you are first learning the basics of the swing, you may ask questions like: "How do I hold the club? Where do I stand? What does a good swing feel like? How far should the backswing go?"

These questions and many like them express the nature of the information about the swing and performance and yet are unknown to the beginner. As the neophyte gradually develops insights into these questions, he or she begins to develop a personal reference system that includes this information. In fact, as the learning process progresses, the learner stores data concerning essential visual, audio and kinesthetic components of the golf swing.

Each expression about the learner's questions refers to the reference system that learners develop within themselves. This reference system assists the individual in determining for himself the correctness of his performance. Let's use the term "model of correct performance" to indicate this reference system that is more valuable when developed through **self-discovery** feedback than from KR.

Efficient training provides information (basic core information) to students that will provide them with the opportunity to develop their own correct performance reference system. This information is especially vital early in the early steps of making progress. In fact, at this point it is much more important than later in the learning process. Thus, an efficient playful learning environment will support the nature of the learning process well enough to help students experience long term progress.

A primary reason beginners can have difficulty in performing a new skill is because of their inability to determine for themselves what their errors are. An important element of making progress is the development by the student of an internalized model of a workable outcome. This model is formulated by golfers matching their own sensory feedback information about their performance with the feedback information that the individual receives concerning his or her performance. Hopefully, during practice the student begins to become less dependent on the KR information and is able to depend more on information that he or she has stored in his own internal model. When playing golf every swing is different, with a new adjustment for each different shot. The swing model comes from the current conditions of the shot that is being played.

How much KR or error information should be presented to the learner? At one end of the continuum you have the problem of not enough information, while at the other end you have an equally perplexing problem of too much information.

T. Smoll showed that there is obviously a point of diminishing returns, that is, providing the student with more precise KR may not be as beneficial as one might expect. ***A study revealed that too***

precise KR not only may be of limited, if any, help to the student; it may actually be detrimental to learning.

The information which a student can use changes as the learning proceeds. Ammons states that "learning is, in fact, dependent upon the subject's acquisition of techniques for utilizing a greater range of information." It is very important for sports skill instructors to understand the principle relating to KR in the precision and stages of learning. What you tell a beginner may be information too specific for a beginner to use, while for the skilled performer, the same information is very helpful. **A far too common error is to provide beginners with KR information about their performance which should be reserved for advanced performers.**

Each time you hit a golf ball during a practice session, three time intervals become important to you.

- First, there is the time interval from when you have finished hitting the ball until feedback gives you information; this is the pre-KR interval.
- The second is the time that elapses from the instructor giving you that information until you swing again: the post-KR interval.
- Finally, you can consider the entire time between hitting one practice ball and hitting another ball: the inter-response interval.

These three periods of time are important to you because it is during these intervals that you have the opportunity to use the information you have received both from your own feedback systems and from KR. Essentially, these intervals are the periods of time in which you process information about your performance.

To consider the KR feedback intervals is to apply memory research to the learning situation. Some recent research has shown that video KR delay (after the lesson) may help performance; it may also affect other aspects of the student's activity which are not revealed by his performance scores. For example, in a particular trial, the person's confidence and what he feels about his own error seem to be related to delay KR.

In conclusion, we find, regarding the pre-KR interval, that not giving the KR immediately or letting the learner do some other activity helps to learn the task.

Some studies indicate that verbal activity during the post-video-KR interval affects learning. **This activity *interferes* with learning the task, especially early in learning.** Thus, it appears that determining what to do with the feedback received is the process instructors and/or students are interfering with, when there is verbal activity directly following the video-KR. What are the implications for instruction concerning KR?

We must be certain that *the information and the amount of information provided* to the student following a response is *the kind he or she can use* to make some adjustment in their next response (purely visual without words). This information must be limited to the amount of similar and dissimilar information the student can actually use.

Training (Time on Task)

The amount of training affects the quality of learning, although the effect is not always proportional. If a golfer wants to become a better putter, it seems only reasonable that he or she be encouraged to spend as much time as possible on the practice putting green. ***But this is not always the case.***

When a person practices a motor skill, is it possible that the individual reaches a point of **diminishing returns**. What are the benefits derived from the practice in relation to the amount of time put into the practice? This *benefits vs. time* question is an important consideration that motor skills instructors should not overlook in designing instruction.

The term "over-learning" is the focus of a specific area of study that addresses how much practice is beneficial to assure the optimum amount of progress (time spent for benefits received). Over-learning is practice time spent beyond the amount of practice time needed to achieve some performance criteria.

The golfer who is trying to improve his putting skills needs to establish some criteria goals for his or her own practice time. After these criteria are reached, practice should not cease. However, the practice that follows the achievement of those criteria should conform to two guidelines.

- Practice putting with the same intensity as before for only a short period of time to reinforce the learning.
- Putting practice should continue, but not with the intensity of practice time as before.

First, train the skill to reinforce the learning that has taken place (not for new learning). Continue practicing the skill, **but for a greatly reduced amount of time.**

The spacing or distribution of practice appears to affect performance rather than learning. It can be difficult to decide how to organize the time available in a practice session or practice period. Students are concerned with accomplishing as much as possible in the available time, but if that time is not used wisely, much of it is wasted. **Massed practice** is practice where the amount of rest between trials is either very short or nonexistent, making practice relatively continuous.

Distributed practice is practice in which the amount of rest between trials or groups is relatively large. The "mass vs. distributed practice schedule" controversy should not be a controversy at all. The evidence seems convincing that distributed practice is superior to massed practice as a contribution to actual performance.

The decision to practice a motor skill as a whole or in parts should be made on the basis of the complexity and organization of the skill. An important decision you must make when learning any motor skill will be the one on how you practice the skill. Should the skill be practiced in its entirety or by parts? The issue of whole vs. part practice has been a topic of discussion in the motor learning literature since the early part of this century. If the skill is high in complexity but low in organization the practice of parts would be recommended. But, if the skill is low in complexity and high in organization (golf swing), practice of the whole or entire skill would be the better choice.

What parts will be practiced separately and what parts will be combined? That is, those parts of a skill which are highly dependent on each other should be practiced together as a unit, but those parts which are relatively independent can be practiced individually.

A swing, ball contact, and follow-through are strongly interdependent; these components should always be practiced as a complete unit. Just because the components are independent does not mean they must be practiced independently, it only means they can be. **Studies suggest that the golf swing should be trained as a complete unit.**

Variability of practice is important for motor skills where novel responses must be made. The chances are probably rather low that you had actually practiced every response which may have to be made, because of the vast number of possible conditions or situations that can occur.

A **novel response** is defined as a situation in which the response to be made has not been previously performed in exactly the same way that it must be made in the situation confronting the performer. **This is applicable to golf as every shot has a unique set of circumstances.**

Richard Schmidt published an article in *Psychological Review* entitled "Schema theory of discrete motor skill learning." Schmidt theorized that when an individual makes a motor response, he abstracts four factors from that response and stores them in memory: Initial conditions, Response specifications, Sensory consequences, and Response outcome. According to Schmidt, these four sources of information are stored together after a movement is made. Eventually, the individual develops a "schema" for that movement or movement type, on the basis of the information that has been abstracted during the practice trials.

Schmidt indicates that the probability of being successful in a novel response situation can also be directly related to the practice that the individual had experienced prior to the novel response situation.

Thus, the chances of responding correctly on any given shot will be in large measure related to the nature of the training that precede that shot.

It is important that the practice conditions for motor skills include novel-response situations that include a great deal of variety. This variety of practice situations should be combined with an adequate amount of practice. **A constant golf swing is the misguided aim of many golfers.** Every swing they will have to make when playing has to be different. Preparing for these novel response situations requires that practice conditions be characterized by

(1) An adequate amount of practice of the basic movement.

(2) A variety of situations in which the movement will be used.

Practice that occurs mentally can be beneficial to the acquisition of a new motor skill and to the performance of a well-learned skill. Situations in which mental practice can be applied abound in motor skills. These situations range from employing mental practice to help learn a new skill, to using it to assist in the performance of an activity at a world-class competitive event.

Research investigations of the relationship between mental practice and physical performance can be traced to the 1890s, while *philosophic* discussions can be traced back to Plato and beyond. When the term mental practice is used in research literature, it refers to the cognitive rehearsal of a physical skill in the absence of overt, physical movements. An individual is involved in mental practice when he or she imagines actually performing a skill, or part of a skill. No involvement of the body's musculature is noticed by an observer.

For Example:

One group only practiced the task physically each day.

A second group practiced physically with three out of every four trials, beginning with a mental practice trial.

A third group alternated mental and physical practice trials during each session.

The fourth group practiced physically during only one of every group of four trials, while practicing mentally during the other trials.

Oxendine concluded from these results that a proper combination of mental practice and physical practice can be as valuable as physical practice alone. In the experiment, that proportion was at least 50% of each type of practice.

During mental practice, the individual is actually producing action currents in the muscle groups (and in the brain) that are used in the physical movement. The associated sensory feedback is also produced, thus allowing the person to make appropriate adjustments for the next imagined practice attempt. Another possible explanation relates the effectiveness of mental practice to learning theory and to memory theory.

Mental practice can help the learner answer some of the questions that characterize the early stage of learning, without the learner being pressured to simultaneously physically perform the skill. In the later stages of learning, mental practice would seem to be beneficial in assisting the learner to consolidate strategies as well as to correct errors.

Imagery, as you will recall, is considered to be a primary means of encoding movement information for storage in memory. On this basis, the use of imagery in mental practice would facilitate the storage of the movement in memory.

Students who are waiting their turn can mentally practice a certain number of movements or exercises. *How* the mental practice is performed is important. **The students should imagine themselves doing the skill correctly.** This imagining can include the entire skill or a specific part of the skill that is being worked on. Following these guidelines for implementing mental practice, students should go through this procedure a specified number of times, such as five or ten mental practices not only keeps inactive students occupied but also provides them with an opportunity to be involved in an activity that will help them learn and encode the skill they are practicing in the brain.

Motivation

Motivation is important to motor skill learning and performance because of its role in the *initiation, maintenance, and intensity of behavior.* Any discussion of motivation should be concerned with determining the causes of a behavior; this in turn involves investigation of what influences those causes. Although motives are defined as being internal, the influences on these inner causes can be external.

Progress and Motivation as Reciprocal

The critical question is whether or not progress can actually occur when an individual is not motivated to learn. At times, the inner desire to learn is not consciously present at the initiation of the situation, but the student can develop an inner desire or motivation to continue. Examples of this type of situation are very common in physical education classes. A student has no choice in becoming involved in the class and yet develops a motivation to play more and to continue to be involved.

Incidental learning. Some progress can occur in the absence of motivation to learn. This appears in situations where incidental learning can be considered. **Research demonstrates that unconscious learning does occur even when the student was not directed to learn.**

Anxiety Affects Learning and Performance

According to the interrelationship between the level of anxiety and the complexity of the task, anxiety affects learning and performance. ***Trait anxiety*** is similar to personality characteristics. It is a person's general predisposition to perceive a situation as threatening or non-threatening. *State anxiety*, on the other hand, is how the individual responds to a situation – it is the emotional state of an individual who experiences feelings of apprehension, tension, nervousness, worry, or fear.

Charles Spielberger (1966) provided a useful analogy to assist in distinguishing between trait and state anxiety. State anxiety is to trait anxiety as kinetic energy is to energy in motion, while trait anxiety is similar to potential energy or energy available for action when the appropriate stimulus appears.

Levels of Anxiety and Performance

Two theories have emerged as the most prominent in attempting to explain the relationship between anxiety and motor performance. Drive theory, developed by Hull (1943) and promoted by Spence (1958), is that a low degree of state anxiety would result in a low performance level, whereas a high state anxiety level would yield a high performance level.

Alternative to this is the *Inverted-U theory*. This theory postulates that both too low and too high levels of anxiety result in similar low performance, while a moderate level of anxiety should yield high performance.

Levels of State Anxiety and the Situation

The trait anxiety characteristics also appear to interact with two very important situational variables, the importance of the situation to the individual and the uncertainty of the outcome of the situation. The more importance an individual ascribes to a situation, the more likely he or she is to develop high levels of state anxiety.

Anxiety and the Task

The Yerkes-Dodson Law relates activation levels to the task to be performed. A similar relationship must be considered for anxiety as well. The two characteristics of motor tasks (task difficulty and task complexity) are important here. It seems quite reasonable that it is the complexity of a task that is more related to the effects of anxiety on performance, than the difficulty of the task.

The golfer who is at the high end of the state anxiety scale while putting undoubtedly can make a poor putt. On the other hand, it would be very advantageous for a power lifter to be located towards the high end of the state anxiety scale.

THE BRAIN
SEE IT and FEEL IT

Key Concepts into Mental Choreography

This segment has been influenced by Steven Brown and Lawrence M. Parson's article in *Scientific American* (2008, July edition).

Progress arrives through a playful and joyful thinking process that requires no specialized retained knowledge or detailed subject matter information. What has been compiled in this segment of *Play Golf to Learn Golf* can leave you with a firm grip on the nature of brain compatible principles for making progress and the process of learning. Fundamental insights that can be lessons for learning and living in everyday life, including making progress in golf.

Investigators suggest that we mentally rehearse what we see. They have found that when people watch physical actions areas in the brain's pre-motor cortex involved in performing those actions switch on. This is a practice that helps us learn and understand new movement. **The key concept here is that what we see is more useful to us than word descriptions.**

The ability to rehearse a movement in your mind is indeed vital to learning motor skills. In 2006, Emily S. Cross, Scott Grafton and their colleagues at Dartmouth College considered whether imitation circuits in the brain increase their activity as learning takes place. The results of their studies confirmed that the activity in the pre-motor cortex increased during training and was correlated to the subject's ability to perform a viewed motion. **The key concept here is a viewed motion.**

Investigations have highlighted the fact that when leaning motor sequence activities (i.e., tennis serves, golf swings, and a dance sequence) our motor planning system that contains information (pictures - feels) about the body's ability to accomplish a specific movement. This information is being used in addition to a direct motor system for the control of muscle contractions. **The key concept is pictures and feels.**

Research shows that the ability to simulate motion sequences in the mind is not only visual, three studies suggest it is kinesthetic as well - see it and feel it. Indeed, true mastery requires a muscle sense and a motor image in the brain's motor planning areas of the movement in question. Visual and feel stimulation is a key ingredient in learning motions.

One brain area houses a representation of the body's orientation, helping to direct our movement through space. There is another area of the brain which serves as a synchronizer of sorts, enabling us to pace our actions. **The key concept is that the whole brain is involved.**

Mature planning occurs in the frontal lobe where the pre-motor cortex and the supplementary motor area evaluate signals from everywhere in the brain, indicating such information as position in space and memories of past actions. Several areas of the brain then communicate with the primary motor cortex, which determines which muscles need to contract and by how much, and then sends instructions down through the spinal cord to the muscles. **The key concept is the past actions.**

The fine-tuning of motions occurs, in part, as the muscles return signals to the brain. The cerebellum uses the sensory feedback from the muscles to help maintain balance and refine movements. In addition, the basal ganglia collect sensory information from critical regions and convey it through the thalamus to motor areas of the cortex. **The key concept is sensory feedback.**

We are sensing the positioning of our torso and limbs at all times, even with your eyes shut, thanks to the muscles' sensory organs. These organs index the rotation of each joint and the tension in each muscle and relay that information to the brain, which generates an articulate body representation in response. **The key concept here is "at all times."**

Many scientists believe that the brain contains a kinesthetic map that permits an awareness of body positioning in space while people navigate through their surroundings. **The key concept here is the kinesthetic mapping.**

The cerebellum as a whole meets the criteria for a good neural metronome, it receives a broad array of sensory inputs from the auditory, visual and sensory areas of the brain (a capability that is necessary to entrain movement) and it contains sensor motor representations for the entire body. **The key concept here is *feel* representations.**

In 1984, I wrote *See and Feel the Inside Move the Outside* and have revised and republished the book three times since then. My continued learning journey reinforces my initial thoughts that the more people rely on seeing a motor pattern and can imagine what the pattern feels like, the more effortless it becomes to carry out the motor skill.

Learning is at the heart of all progress. The first major texts in motor learning appeared in the late 1960s. A student-teacher interaction goes on. It is the teacher who structures the learning setting or environment, and it is the teacher who has the responsibility to understand how a person learns.

A logical place to start is to have some knowledge of what aspects of human behavior involve learning. Learning is involved in a variety of types of behaviors. A convenient tool for classifying human behavior involves using the categories of three domains, namely the cognitive, affective, and motor domain.

Cognitive Domain

Behavior in the cognitive domain involves intellectual activities. There may be as many as 120 human abilities in the cognitive domain.

The organism (brain and body) does many things with information available to it. Such mental operations as discovery or recognition of information (cognition), retention or storage of information (memory), generation of information from given data, and reaching decisions or making judgments about the information are all performed in cognitive domain.

Affective Domain

The word *affect* refers to feelings or emotions. There is a great deal of evidence that indicates that much, if not most of our affective behavior is learned behavior. See the brain, body, and mind as separate or independent, yet acting as a team.

Affective behavior can be classified into six general categories:

(1) Awareness

(2) Willingness to Receive

(3) Responding

(4) Valuing

(5) Organizing

(6) Characterization by a Value

The affective domain of behaviors is a very important one for making progress with golf. We are constantly including in our goals of learning such things as motivation, interest, and respect for others, responsibility, and the like.

Motor Domain

This category is sometimes referred to as the psychomotor domain to reference the involvement of a mental or cognitive component to most motor skills.

Because of the complex nature of most skills, the development of taxonomy in the motor domain has not been as successful as the skills in the cognitive and affective domains. One system of classification, developed by Elizabeth Simpson in 1966, summarized the situation in the following manner:

- Sensory stimulation
- Set
- Guided response
- Mechanism
- Complex overt response
- Adaptation
- Origination

Edwin Fleishman (1970) has proposed another approach to the development of taxonomy of motor behaviors. Simpson's taxonomy is oriented toward the development of educational objectives; Fleishman's approach is directed more toward an analysis of motor abilities.

The cognitive domain involves behaviors that are typically labeled as "intellectual activities." The affective domain includes emotional behavior; the motor or psychomotor domain includes activities that require physical movement.

These categories of behavior are helpful for the development of objectives for progress to help ensure that the overall goals of training are achieved. An understanding of general structures of skills will be most useful to the effective design of playful learning approaches.

When we consider a topic that is relatively new to us, we are immediately confronted with new terminology. As a person begins to be involved in making progress, especially motor learning, that individual will find his knowledge of the subject quite restricted if he does not acquaint himself with some key terms.

Skill

We can define skill as those "acts or tasks that require movement and are learned in order to be performed unconsciously." We define ability as a "general capacity of an individual."

Movement Pattern

A movement pattern involves the basic elements of a particular motor skill; "Series of motor acts which are directed toward accomplishment of some external purpose."

> Learning involves a change in the internal state of a person that must be inferred from the observation of that person's behavior or performance.

Inherent in this role is the need to determine whether or not learning is actually taking place. Two important terms must be introduced in this discussion: learning and performance. An understanding of the distinction between these two terms is essential.

> *Performance* can be thought of most simply as *observable behavior.*

> *Learning* is a phenomenon that is not directly observable; it can only be inferred from a person's behavior or performance.

Improvement in performance resulting from practice should last longer than a short time. Rather, the improvement should continue over a longer period of time. The performance should show increasingly less variability over time.

Learning is defined as a change in the internal state of the individual that is inferred from a relatively permanent improvement in performance as a result of practice.

A *Learning Situation* is one in which the student is attempting to acquire or acquires a new *skill* or attempts to improve or improves a skill.

A *Performance Situation*, in contrast, is one in which the student is performing or using a *skill* rather than practicing it.

Do not become confused by these uses of the terms *learning and performance.*

The four categories of performance measures are:

- Speed
- Accuracy
- Response Magnitude
- Response Latency

Memory

In the central processing mechanism, students take information and determine the plan of attack or strategy for the response in a playful manner. **Several elements comprise this mostly non-conscious process.** One of the major elements is the memory of past experiences. The student has stored in memory various prior responses and their outcomes. Individuals recall from memory what seems relevant. Hence memory is involved in both the storage and retrieval of information.

Not only is memory involved in central processing, but it is also involved in strategy making. What strategies were used in the past and how they worked is retrieved from memory. Then they are used to develop a new strategy for the present situation. New information mixes with and flows through past experiences to encode new learning.

When the decision has been made concerning the appropriate strategy, the brain then organizes the components of the response and sends them on to the muscles for the appropriate response. Efficiency of response is considered here along with the appropriateness of that response. The response chosen will be executed, whether it is correct or incorrect. **The outcome becomes feedback for future use.**

The correctness or incorrectness of the response is fed back to the central processing unit for the sensory systems and stored in memory to be used as a reference the next time. The feedback information is the most important consideration for making progress.

Processing Information

The human performer is constantly processing information in order to successfully learn or perform motor skills.

Consider, by way of application, how the senses or sensory modes are specifically involved in motor skill performance. Vision is obviously an important sensory mode. The auditory sensory mode is another important sense we involve in motor skill performance.

Proprioception is a term being used here to include what has been traditionally called the kinesthetic sense. Proprioceptive information is important to the performer in executing a skill as well as for preparing for the next attempt.

Kinesthesis is a term we will consider as limited to sensation related to the movement of the limbs. Proprioception is used to indicate the sense of the position and movement in space of the body and body parts as well as the forces and pressures on the body or its parts. For example, the golfer often determines how good his swing is by the *feel* of the swing. Golf instructors are trying to help beginners develop a rhythm to *groove* the swing. All this is based on proprioception, since the golfer cannot watch their swing in order to make proper adjustments. Proprioceptors are located in two areas, joints and muscles.

We rely on our visual, auditory, proprioceptive and tactile sensory receptors in the performance or motor skills. Motor skill performance is the product of the interactions of the sensory systems to produce a response. We integrate the information from a variety of sensory sources even though we tend to direct our conscious attention to only one system. The golfer uses vision in the production of the golf swing, as well as proprioceptive information. Each sensory mode is important to the proper execution of the swing.

Our analysis of information from the environment in relation to motor skill performance begins at the sense receptor level. The semantic problem we must resolve involves the distinction between sensation and perception.

Sensation is defined as the activity of sensory receptors and the resulting transmission to the central nervous system.

Perception is the interpretation of sensory information.

The performer's awareness of information available through a specific sensory mode is essential to progress. Attempts to follow directions or think about details fragments sensory awareness. If we consider performance resulting from relying on information from an improper sensory source, we soon become aware of the need to rely on the sensory modality that can provide the best information for the situation. We must recognize which sensory modes are essential to the successful performance of a skill. If the performer relies too heavily on information from other modes, the performance will ultimately suffer.

Vision

Vision is often considered the queen of the senses. We rely on vision as primary source of information. There is also some significant experimental evidence to show how much we rely on vision when it is available, even though it may not be the best source for optimum performance. Some argument could be presented that these experiments deal with the perceptual rather than sensory process. These experiments obviously point to the interrelationship between sensation and perception.

Cross-modal transfer is the transfer of experiencing or learning in one sensory mode to another sensory mode. If you can see while you are moving, how will your response work if you try it without being able to see your response? In this situation you are experiencing in the visual mode and transferring that experience to the proprioceptive mode.

Generally, experimental results indicate that transferring from the visual to the kinesthetic mode leads to more error than the reverse process of transferring from the kinesthetic to the visual.

It seems that we will ignore other sensory modes of information as our primary source when vision is available, even if the other sensory sources are actually more reliable. What this seems to mean for learning motor skills is that one must make a deliberate attempt to induce the learner to rely on the sensory modality most beneficial to the performance of the skill, rather than always relying on vision.

Perception

A basic phase of making progress with a motor skill involves the individual performer to rely on information from their sensory systems that is the most useful information for producing the most effective and efficient response.

Perceptual tasks involve the detection, comparison and recognition of sensory information. Primary perceptual decisions involve the detection of cues.

Comparison decisions compare one stimulus to a standard that is present.

Recognition decisions are tasks that require a decision based on memory of the correct standard required.

When we discuss sensation, we are discussing the entrance of information through the sensory channels or modes. Obviously, motor skill performance cannot occur with any probability of success if no decisions are made about the information received through the senses. We must interpret that information and then determine whether it is useful or necessary for the task being performed or whether it is simply noise.

It might be noted that Ellis (1977) presented five rather than three types of perceptual decisions: *detection*, *discrimination*, *recognition*, *identification*, and *judgment*.

Evidence indicates we can be trained to improve our ability to detect these signals. The training of an athlete to rapidly detect important cues can also have an impact for the individual who may not be as innately gifted with detection acuity as his counterpart. However, through training and practice, the less gifted athlete can sometimes actually surpass the more gifted performer.

Stress affects the individual's ability to detect a signal. If the performer is fatigued - or in contrast, too excited - he may think he is receiving signals that are not actually present or he may not detect signals that are actually there. As a cognitive skill, pattern recognition is vitally important. In the motor domain, we can relate pattern recognition to cue detection.

Pattern recognition is not an effortless process, it is one which requires past experiences. By developing this perceptual ability, the performer greatly increases his chances for success in the performance of complex motor skills. **Training for general non-specific pattern recognition, especially in the form of cue detection, is an essential component of the learning process for any motor skill.** In motor behavior, the ability to recognize patterns on the basis of seeing only a portion of that pattern, or cue, can be a significant advantage to the performer.

Types of Memory

Short-term memory, or immediate memory, is quite distinct from sensory memory. This differentiation is based on temporal as well as functional criteria. The temporal distinction is that sensory storage occurs **first**. The functional distinction is that sensory storage (the image of what has been seen) is maintained only long enough for the "encoding" of the visual shapes into meaningful components to take place. **That is, we maintain the image in visual sensory storage only until we have made some "usable sense" out of it.**

Sensory memory is the stage of memory that represents a subtle shift from perception to memory. If sensory memory appears to be more a perceptual process than a memory process, it is only because memory begins with the reception of information, which is perception itself. "How much can be seen in a single brief exposure?"

What is "stored" in this memory is "read" from the memory, just as if the stimulus were still active. While the football quarterback views the defense very rapidly, he actually "sees" portions of what he observed for a longer period of time than the time of his active visual scan. He can see that information while it is in storage in the sensory memory. However, this information will only be available for about one second, which should be enough time for him to make whatever cognitive decision is necessary.

What is stored in the sensory memory is a visual image or representation of what has been briefly viewed. Based on what we now know about sensory memory the primary concern, for those in the roll as motor skill instruction, is "keying" the performer to look for specific cues in an array of cues. **The player will ultimately perform better if he "keys" on certain cues in the fast changing environment, in contrast to trying to observe visually and to comprehend all the information available (less can be more).**

Attention and Memory

In motor behavior, timing is an essential ingredient of successful performance. This concept of timing is referred to as *anticipation timing.*

What seems important here is that a critical point in a movement demands attention or processing capacity (the start and finish of a golf swing). Such a critical phase would seem to be any point in the movement that requires some decision to be made concerning the next part of the movement. This decision could involve a change in speed, direction, force, tempo, contact with an external object, or some other modification

We do not have the ability to attend to more than one thing at a time even if two or more tasks require our processing capacity or attention. **During the production of a movement, it appears that not all of that movement requires our attention. For any task at any level of performance, the initiation of the movement demands attention.**

Attention directed toward other aspects of the skill during this initiation phase will probably cause performance of the movement to be poorer than otherwise expected.

Rather than attending to any phase of a stroke, a player should develop a clear visual image of the results and then simply "let it happen." Attention is redirected from the how-to-do-it aspects of the stroke to the image of where the player wants the club and the ball to go. This type of advice is a good example of attending to the beginning phase and termination phase of a movement. In this example, **all the mechanics do not demand attention.**

Results of experiments indicate that for simple, discrete movements, attention or processing capacity is required to begin and to end the movement. The full execution phase of the movement does not require processing capacity.

Selective Attention

How can we select certain information or cues and ignore others? What kinds of cues do we pay attention to, and what clues should we observe?

The study of selective attention is the third area of concentration in our total discussion of attention. Thus far, attention has been considered as alertness and as relating to processing capacity. When a complex array of stimuli is visually presented to a person, he or she is much more able to report with accuracy the characteristics of stimuli that he or she was *directed* to observe, as opposed to those which he or she was not instructed to observe.

All signals excite their stored representations in memory; that is, **they activate what has been placed in memory from the indirect preparation of previous experiences.** However, the system only selects information for further processing that it considers to be most pertinent, based on expectations and the perceptual process. Our brain will only select that information from the environment that we consider the most pertinent, or relevant, to the situation (survivor skills). As you can see, the importance of **previous experience** and instruction concerning essential cues becomes critical for all motor skills instructors.

Memory Conclusions

We can draw at least three conclusions:

First, attend to only one cue in the midst of many competing cues. Golfers can learn to ignore the many irrelevant cues or distractions that will confront them in most situations.

Second, we conclude that the brain will attend to the cues that are most meaningful or pertinent to him or her in a particular situation. *The golfer needs insights that indicate what cues are important.* To ignore this important aspect of progress is to invite less than optimum performances. (Refer to the Critical vs. Beneficial evaluation form in Chapter Seven.)

Finally, we know distractions can and do occur. This fact seems to indicate that the training should provide the golfer with ample playful practice in concentrating on the most pertinent or meaningful cues. Eventually the number of possible distractions (a list of details) should decrease as the most meaningful cues are more and more reinforced in the golfer. Another reason for distractions seems to be the learner's lack of confidence that the cues he or she is attending to are the most pertinent. It is essential to develop confidence in attending to those cues.

Memory is an important component (if not the most important) in our processing of information in order to produce a desired response.

Motor memory and *verbal memory* are expressions that seem to imply that motor and verbal memory are separate entities. Let's consider the memory for motor skills and for verbal skills.

Retention and *forgetting* are both essential to the understanding of human memory. **Retention and forgetting are influenced by emotion.**

Memory must be considered from the point of view of its structure and control processes. Structure involves fixed, permanent features that maintain their characteristics or traits, regardless of the task.

Control processes, on the other hand, refer to those processes of memory that are under the individual's direct control (such as storage of information, rehearsal, or retrieval of information).

If the subject briefly views information, or if he or she directs attention only to the physical characteristics of the information *without meaning*, then the depth or level of processing would be very shallow. This would be the case if you look at a word and make no attempt to determine its meaning; you simply acknowledge what it looks like. *On the other hand, if the individual processes the information to the extent that he or she associates the new information with what he or she already knows, then the depth or level of processing is very deep.* Shallow processing would be similar to the sensory or short-term stores, whereas deep processing would be related to the long-term store.

Our immediate ability to use information just presented to us, such as a telephone number from the information operator, or instructions on a serve in tennis, comes from storage of that information in the short-term stage. Motor or kinesthetic information is lost quite rapidly in the short-term store. Information that we do not process further - or rehearse - is lost.

We tend to lose information (forget) from short-term storage after only about 20 to 30 seconds. We are not only concerned with how long information will remain in short-term storage, but also how much information we can accommodate there. We have the capacity to hold about seven items (plus or minus two items) such as words or digits, in short-term storage. The larger item requires processing of information beyond the short-term storage stage.

The duration and the capacity of long-term storage of information are described as infinite and unlimited. One means of transferring information into long-term storage is playful rehearsal of the information. This process provides a means of processing the information to such a degree that it becomes more resistant to loss or oblivion.

This infinite duration and capacity of long-term storage does not imply there is no forgetting. Forgetting seems to be more a question of retrieval, rather than a problem of not having the information available in long-term storage. We seem to be unable to find the location where we have stored the information (unless joined with a past event.)

When you are given skill instruction, what aspects of the movements in these skills do you remember or try to remember? How do you make yourself remember what is important for the proper execution of these skills? Do you select certain phases of each skill and in some way concentrate on remembering these? Do you try to combine the new instruction and past practice experiences you have had? Each of these questions points to an important aspect of the study of human memory - that is, *control processes*. When information makes sense and has meaning, it is remembered. Making sense and having personal meaning are not the same.

Sports and Memory

In sports skills, we are learning movement patterns and sequences. This learning requires unconscious memory. Let's discuss some of the problems that arise in attempting to determine how students store, organize, and use the information they have received through a particular sensory modality.

Control processes are important in the study of human memory, for they represent the means by which we operate or use our memories. They are under our direct control and immediately influence the remembering or forgetting of information.

The effective use of control processes depends greatly on how the learner is instructed to remember, what kind of task is being learned, and past experiences of the learner. Poor memory is due in large measure to our own lack of the effective use of the control processes at our disposal.

The selection and transfer of particular portions of presented information comprise one form of the control process in the sensory register; what should be transferred to the short-term storage system; and what should be processed further.

Another control process is one's decision determining which sensory channel to attend to. Each of these control processes is under the direct control of the student; therefore, it will have significant impact on what information is stored in memory, and how it is stored.

Storage, organization, and retrieval - these three control processes in memory are especially important to our understanding of memory.

Playfully encoding information is a major strategy in memory involved in the storage of information. For storage purposes, we seem to be able to most effectively use those aspects of verbal information which relate to how the information sounds, what it means, or the image it projects.

Movement has many characteristics we could encode in memory. We might consider the spatial position of various points of a movement, **such as the beginning and the end point of a golf swing.** We could also encode the distance of the movement, its velocity, its force, or the direction of the movement. *Research indicates that location information is better encoded than distance.* When location information is highly reliable, subjects tend to base their distance movements on that information. However, when location information is very unreliable, the subject will base their movement on the rate or velocity of the movement.

In practical terms, location points of the golf club are phases of progress that beginning students should know. Training should keep golfers engaged in this element of progress. **The key elements of the swing are the beginning point of the swing, and a location cue about the finish of the swing.**

Feel and Memory

Where is the encoded kinesthetic information stored? There are two possible locations. One is central in the brain itself, while the other storage location may be peripheral, that is, in the proprioceptors. We would expect that information coded and stored in the central memory store would be more resistant to spontaneous decay than would peripherally stored information.

An inference when two modes of storing information are used: location information is stored centrally, but distance information is stored peripherally.

How do we code kinesthetic information? We store images, or pictorial representations of spatial location information. **We store location information in a visual-kinesthetic code, but we store distance information in a kinesthetic code.**

Organization Memory

Organization

There is little dispute that we group and categorize information we intend to learn. Research demonstrates how the organization of movement occurs and how this organization affects performance.

Unfortunately, beginners tend to consider motor skills as comprised of many parts. As the beginner develops his or her ability to execute a skill, the number of components of the skill seems to decrease. This does not mean the structure of the skill itself has changed. Rather, the student's view of the learning environment has changed. Three or four component parts are now being considered as one. The result will eventually be the learner's ability to perform the entire routine with the proper and requisite timing. Rhythm and coordination are necessary.

You can facilitate learning a complex skill by encouraging students to practice the skill as a whole that fits into a logical organization. The scheme should be based on the patterning and flow of the parts. *Portions of the routine that require the previous parts to begin or the next part to continue should be practiced as a complete unit.* Practice the routine by following a logical organizational scheme of **the whole motion**, thus aiding the retrieval process in memory, which in turn facilitates learning the routine.

Forgetting

Lost information in memory is usually called forgetting. But we are often confronted with the problem that all information that is lost from memory may not be forgotten. It may be simply misplaced and waiting to be located. What is perplexing; however, are the causes of forgetting. Forgetting is not only a very important theoretical issue in the study of human memory but also a critical, practical phenomenon. **If we can anticipate not only what, but why students forget in the process of learning motor skills, we can begin to arrange the presentation of instructional information to conform to this knowledge of why forgetting occurs.**

One of the earliest investigations of time as a possible cause of forgetting in motor memory was the Adams and Dijkstra (1966) study. The amount of errors the subjects made increased steadily as the length of the retention interval increased, with 20 seconds appearing as the point in time when the amount of error was appreciably different from almost immediate recall - that is, 5 seconds. We can be rather certain that when kinesthetic information is put into short-term storage, it is susceptible to the effects of time. Following a period of 20-30 seconds, that information begins to be lost fairly rapidly **when it does not make sense or has no meaning.**

Only in short-term storage does trace decay appear to be a cause of forgetting. Long-term storage of information appears to be influenced primarily by interfering activity, which of course interacts with time. For example, if you try to recall a gymnastic routine after several years of not having performed it, you will have some initial difficulty remembering all the varied aspects of the routine. While it is obvious that time is a factor here, we must consider the possible interfering influences of the many verbal and motor tasks you have performed since you last performed the routine you wish to recall. It is important to remember, however, *that long-term storage* is not a temporary depository of information, but instead a relatively *permanent storage place*, where information seems to be misplaced rather than to decay. **Memory of poor habits does not leave the brain, and they can be sign posts for developing new habits. Trying to change or fix a poor outcome is a negative approach to progress.** Fixing isn't learning.

Focusing on what to do is more useful than focusing on what not to do, or how to do it

Interference

Experts on memory generally accept interference as one cause of forgetting.

Proactive interference. There seems to be relatively convincing evidence that proactive or before- interference effects are a reason for forgetting kinesthetic information in short-term storage. Evidence indicates that if we store the movement to-be-recalled as a verbal symbol, such as when we use counting and or numbers to help recall movement, then verbal activity can be a cause of forgetting. Just feel or see it.

It appears that we can quite readily overcome proactive interference effects by actively rehearsing the information after it is learned. This means that by active practice of the movement, we strengthen the trace for the movement in memory and thus notice little, if any, effects of proactive interference. If the interfering verbal activity occurs during the retention interval, we will generally observe poorer recall than if no activity had occurred.

It would appear then that while retroactive or after-interference effects are observed in motor memory, the activity that causes the interference must be relatively demanding for the subject. Another way of expressing this idea would be to say that the activity must be attention demanding for the subject.

Another motor activity, especially if it is relatively similar to the one you are trying to remember, will produce more interference than verbal activity. This implies that if the student moves with a model (such as swinging the golf club as the instructor demonstrates), the accuracy attempting to reproduce that movement will be greater provided no other related movement is performed in between the demonstration and the practice attempt. Instructors should try to make certain that when they are going through a series of movements they have their students practice the movements they are emphasizing as close in time to the demonstration as possible.

Learning approaches should allow students to practice the swing they just made along with you before introducing any variations.

The influence of time or interference on memory is related to how deeply the person has processed the information. With regard to forgetting, this approach implies that forgetting, or conversely recall, can be directly attributed to the level of processing of the information by the individual. That is, if only physical features of an object were noted, then there will be a higher probability of forgetting than if the individual had stored information about how the object was related to some object already stored in memory.

Researchers have considered the role of verbal labels for movements (from students) as a means of processing the movement at a deeper level than when no such designation is used. In subjects who were presented with a movement along with their own relevant verbal label, less forgetting occurred than when no label was provided.

Learning to hit a golf ball or to serve a tennis ball are examples of sport skills that require the performer to combine movements in a specified arrangement. In any of these situations, if the order of performing the component actions is not followed the final outcome often will not be the desired one.

The following categories describe very common, practical problems in which memory processes are involved:

Primacy-recency effect. This is seen when a person recalls verbal items in series, such as words or numbers. Those items that were *first presented* to the person, that is, the early portion of the list, and those that were presented last, the *end portion* of the list, are usually recalled better than items in the middle of the list.

Primacy-recency effect exists in the motor domain as well as in the verbal domain. Several studies have reported that recall of a series of movements did not follow the same laws, as did the recall of a series of words. Instead, it appears that movement series were recalled with a primacy effect only, that is, early movements were recalled best and end movements were not recalled as well.

What does all of this have to tell us about learning in motor skills? When learning a routine, you are in a serial memory situation. You are immediately confronted with questions relating to the order of presentation of each of the movements or components of the routine that needs to be emphasized. Students will have difficulty remembering what to do in the middle portions of the entire routine. **They will probably recall most readily the first and last portions of the routine. Thus, golfers should be prepared to emphasize the start and finish portions of their swing to encourage practicing and learning the feel of these movements first.**

Neuro-Muscular System

The control of movement is dependent on the structure and function of the neuro-muscular system.

When we make any movement, the musculature involved in the action has received direct commands from the central nervous system. What nerves were activated to carry the message instructing the muscles to move? Where did the message originate and how was it transmitted? Once the movement begins, how is it kept going? How is the brain involved in learning and controlling movement?

How the body is involved in controlling its own movement is indeed intriguing. Study of the learning and performance of motor skills would be incomplete if the underlying neuro-muscular system were ignored.

The most basic component of the neuro-muscular system is the neuron, or nerve cell. The nerve cells in the nervous system number in the billions. Although there are several different types of neurons, all share a relatively identical structure. This includes three parts, namely (1) the cell body; (2) dendrites; and (3) axon.

The cell body contains the all-important nucleus. The nucleus regulates the homeostasis of the neuron. Dendrites are nerve fibers that extend from the cell body and are primarily responsible for receiving information from other *neurons*. A neuron may have none or as many as thousands of dendrites. The axon is also a nerve fiber, but it is responsible only for the sending of information from the neuron.

The control of movement involves a highly complex system of peripheral and central nervous system structures. Movement control involves the sensory reception of information concerning the movement to be produced and the integration of the sensory and motor information in order to produce coordinated movement. **Sensory information involved in the control of movement comes from a variety of sources.** Of primary importance to our discussion are the proprioceptors, which are the peripheral sensory receptors in the muscles, the joints, ligaments and tendons. The initiation and control of movement appears to be centered in the cerebral cortex and in the cerebellum, in an intricate and complex control system.

The "closed-loop" theory of motor control maintains that coordinated movement is the result of a linking together of discrete sequences of movements. Each link in this chain of movements is produced from available sensory feedback information from each preceding link. Each motor response or output is the product of commands from the CNS (central nervous system) based on the feedback from the preceding movement. Thus, before a movement sequence occurs, sensory information from the muscles and joints from the preceding movement sequence must be processed before the next movement can be produced.

The "open-loop" or centralist theory of motor control maintains that feedback is not necessary for the control of movement. Movement is controlled by higher centers of the CNS that contain the information necessary to control a complex movement from beginning to end. Thus, no information need be passed on from link to link in a chain of movements. Instead, the central processing system contains all the information necessary to begin and control all the parts of the movement. Most support in favor of the open-loop theory has come from research where the skills involved are ballistic-type skills (i.e., golf swing).

The closed-loop theory seems especially applicable to slow, self-paced type of movements. In these movements, feedback seems to be important in the production of each phase of the total movement. On the other hand, the open-loop theory seems well suited to explain the production of rapid, ballistic-type responses, which the closed-loop theory does not appear to explain very satisfactorily. Glencross (1977) suggested that the issue of motor control should not be an either/or issue. Rather, the two theories should be integrated to provide a comprehensive theory that explains motor control on the basis of the type of movement produced.

Note: Kinesthetic reaction time (RT) studies show that error can be corrected (by feel) in 60 milliseconds. An error can be detected, analyzed and corrected in less time than it would normally take a person to notice the stimulus, and respond to it.

Stephen Keele (1968) defined a motor program as "a set of muscle commands that are structured before a movement sequence begins, and allows the entire sequence to be carried out uninfluenced by peripheral feedback." Keele emphasized in his discussion of this definition that the motor program is not a movement, but rather it acts to control movements. Even in the presence of sensory feedback, the movement is carried out in accordance with the predetermined commands.

Richard Schmidt (1976) defined the motor as "a set of pre-structured alpha and gamma motor commands that, when activated, result in movement oriented toward a given goal, with these movements unaffected by peripheral feedback indicating the goal should be changed."

What seems to be the general consensus, then, is that the motor program is a set of commands from the CNS to the musculature, to perform a given movement. Further, the set of commands will be carried out completely, even if the sensory feedback system indicates midway through the movement that the movement should be altered.

One line of evidence to consider here is that concerning the concept of attention or limited processing capacity. If we really program movements, then we should not have to give our conscious attention to them - that is, use our processing capacity in order to perform them.

In effect, then, the gymnast has programmed movements to be run off in computer program fashion whenever the command occurs, which is the first movement in the unit. The program continues unaffected by sensory feedback until the end of the unit, or last movement. There are certain movement situations that apparently can be explained only by the motor program notion. One of these situations is the performance of a ballistic movement, such as throwing and swinging.

Pre-planning or using a motor program is essential, since the movement seems to be too rapid to be carried out on the basis of peripheral feedback obtained during the movement itself. The second situation involves a series of individual movements that must be performed as a whole unit. Programming these movements is beneficial, so that the individual movements can be coordinated in a smooth, rhythmic fashion without having to depend on sensory feedback as the basis for beginning each individual movement (a golf swing).

Personal Differences

People seem to differ in their ability to learn motor skills. These differences are distinctly evident in a class where a physical activity is being learned by beginners. Consider, for example, a beginning golf class. As you observe the members of that class on the first day when they are permitted to hit the ball, you will see various degrees of success and failure. Some students will spend an inordinate amount of time simply trying to make contact with the ball. At the other extreme, there will be those who seem to hit the ball rather consistently. The remainder of the class is usually distributed somewhere along the continuum of success between those two extremes.

One question we feel compelled to ask is why students exhibit such a wide range of initial ability in a physical activity. Are these differences due to genetic factors or are they attributable to the range of each student's previous experiences with physical activities?

People have a limited ability to store information in memory for a short period of time. Of those who have investigated human motor abilities, one of the most successful has been Edwin Fleishman. He identified such abilities as follows:

(1) Multi-limb coordination;

(2) Control precision;

(3) Response orientation;

(4) Reaction time;

(5) Speed of arm movement;

(6) Rate control;

(7) Manual dexterity;

(8) Finger dexterity;

(9) Arm-hand steadiness;

(10) Wrist, finger speed;

(11) Aiming.

"Physical proficiency abilities" identified by Fleishman are

(1) Static strength;

(2) Dynamic strength;

(3) Explosive strength;

(4) Trunk strength;

(5) Extent flexibility;

(6) Dynamic flexibility;

(7) Gross body coordination;

(8) Gross body equilibrium; and

(9) Stamina.

Why do individuals differ from each other in their motor abilities? **The limited literature available seems to indicate that both genetics and experience are involved in determining the level of ability an individual possesses.** Most motor behavior theorists maintain that motor abilities are more genetically than experience-determined. That is, the ultimate ability level of an individual is controlled primarily by genetic factors. You must be careful in what you conclude from such a statement, however. Do not assume that two individuals cannot achieve similar levels of proficiency in a physical skill because of genetically-determined ability differences.

During the early attempts at learning to perform a complex motor task, spatial awareness-related abilities are significantly related to performance of that task. However, during later practice trials, spatial abilities become less important, while kinesthetic awareness abilities are highly related to performance.

Have you ever been puzzled by the person who appears to be an all-around athlete? Are they born with some special motor ability which enables them to be successful at all they do? Do they learn quicker than others, or are they naturally better at the sports in which they participate?

The basis of the general motor ability hypothesis maintains that there exists in individuals a singular, global motor ability. There is very little evidence reported in the research literature to support the General Motor Ability Hypothesis. There are many motor abilities and these abilities are relatively independent. **This implies that, given a certain level of ability in one motor ability, it would be impossible to state with any confidence what a person's ability level might be in a different motor ability.** It appears that the only justified conclusion is that motor abilities are specific in nature. There seem to be many different motor abilities that are quite independent of each other. Thus, the exact nature and scope or even the existence - of so-called "general motor ability" can be seriously questioned.

If motor abilities are numerous and independent, then how does one person become so proficient at several sports?

Since every individual possesses some degree of each of the various motor abilities that have been identified, it seems reasonable to assume that these abilities could be characterized by a continuum of amounts or levels within each person. The continuum could be anchored at the ends by a low level at one extreme and a high level at the other extreme for each ability. The greater the number of abilities that appeared toward the high level end of the amount of continuum, the higher would be the probability of success in a larger number of sport activities. The so-called all-around-athlete is a rare individual. However, he or she can be explained as a person possessing a high degree of more abilities than the average.

One further issue related to the study of motor abilities is a concept that in the past has been referred to as "motor educability," is the ease with which an individual learns new motor skills.

In the research literature, correlations between motor abilities and motor educability were consistently low, indicating little relationship between a student's motor educability score and the ease with which he or she learned a sport skill. **The important factors in learning are information, motivation, reinforcement, and a safe, smart learning environment as we play to learn.**

To Be Continued...

We never know what the future holds, especially when it comes to what may be possible. I know I will keep looking!

Best of luck pursuing your goals.

Michael Hebron

Suggested Reading and Viewing

Video

Seeing with the Mind's Eye (BBC) Presented by Susan A. Greenfield

Books

Abandoned Generation, The (1995) . . . . William Willimon & Thomas Naylor

Absorbent Mind, The . . . . Maria Montessori

Against School Reform (2002). . . . . Peter S. Temes

Ageless Body, Timeless Mind . . . . Deepak Chopra

Aims of Education, The . . . . Alfred North Whitehead

All I Really Need to Know, I Learned in Kindergarten (1993) . . . . Robert Fulghum

American Ideas and Education (1964) . . . . Frederick Mayer

Ancient Engineers, The (1960). . . . . L. Sprague de Camp

Animals in Translation (2005) . . . . .Temple Grandin & Catherine Johnson

Arts and the Creation of Mind, The (2002) . . . . .Elliot W. Eisner

Art of Awareness, The . . . . Deb Curtis & Margie Carter

Art of Being, The . . . . Erich Fromm

Becoming a "Wiz" at Brain-Based Teaching. . . . . Marilee Sprenger

Between Parent and Child . . . . Dr. Haim G. Ginott

Birth of the Mind, The (2004) . . . . Gary Marcus

Book of Life, The. . . . . .Stephen Jay Gould

Book, The (1966). . . . . Alan Watts

Brain Facts (2000). . . . . Joseph Carey

Brain for All Seasons, A . . . . William H. Calvin

Brief History of the Mind, A . . . . William H. Calvin

Child's Conception of the World, The . . . . Jean Piaget & Jacques Voneche

Children Teach Children. . . . . Alan Gartner, Mary Kohler & Frank Reissman

Cognitive Neuroscience (The Biology of the Mind)
. . . . Michael S. Gazzaniga, Richard B. Ivry & George R. Mangun

Complete Idiot's Guide to Philosophy, The . . . . Jay Stevenson, Ph.D.

Consistency . . . . Adolfo Critto

Construction of Reality in the Child, The . . . . Jean Piaget

Continuum Concept, The. . . . . Jean Liedloff

Control Theory in the Classroom (1986) . . . . William Glasser M.D.

Cooperative Learning . . . . Dana Grisham & Paul Molinelli

Core Transformation. . . . . .Connierae & Tamara Andreas

Correspondence and Memoir (1829) Vols. I–IV. Thomas Jefferson

Crash Course: A Radical Plan for Improving Public Education . . . . Chris Whittle

Creative Power. . . . . .Hughes Mearns

Creative Visualization . . . . Neville Drury

Curriculum (Readings in the Philosophy of Education). . . . . Martin Levit

Dancing Wu Li Masters, The: An Overview of the New Physics . . . . Gary Zukav

Descent of Man, The (1871). . . . . Charles Darwin

Development of Play, The . . . . David Cohen

Dewey on Education (1959). . . . . Martin S. Dworkin

Different Kind of Teacher, A . . . . John Taylor Gatto

Dining in the Raw . . . Rita Romano

Disciplined Mind, The . . . Howard Gardner

Discover Your Genius . . . Michael K. Gelb

Discovery Of The Child, The . . . Maria Montessori

Dominance Factor, The . . . Carla Hannaford, M.D.

Double Helix of Education and the Economy, The . . . Sue E. Berryman & Thomas R. Bailey

Dr. Montessori's Own Handbook . . . Maria Montessori

Dumbing Us Down . . . John Taylor Gatto

E=MC^2, A Biography of the World's Most Famous Equation . . . David Bodanis

Eating for Optimum Health . . . Andrew Weil

Educated Child, The . . . William J. Bennett

Education and the Good Life (1926) . . . Bertrand Russell

Education at the Crossroads . . . Jacques Maritain

Education for Thinking (2005) . . . Deanna Kuhn

Einstein Almanac, The . . . Alice Calaprice

Emotional Intelligence . . . Daniel Goleman

English Reader, The . . . Lindley Murray

Enriching the Brain (2006) . . . Eric Jensen

Experience and Education . . . John Dewey

Extraordinary Golf: The Art of the Possible . . . Fred Shoemaker

Fires in the Bathroom (2003) . . . Kathleen Cushman

Fiscal Readiness for Stress of Change . . . Paul Mort

Fit For Life II: Living Health . . . Harvey & Marilyn Diamond

Food Revolution, The . . . John Robbins

Frogs into Princes . . . Richard Bandler

From Conception to Birth: A Life Unfolds . . . Alexander Tsiaras & Barry Werth

Games (1909) . . . Jessie H. Bancroft

Golfing Machine, The . . . Homer Kelley

Great Game of Business, The . . . . Jack Stack & Bo Burlingham

Guide to Reading Piaget, A . . . . Molly Brearley & Elizabeth Hitchfield

Guiding Free Expression in Children's Art . . . . Helen Merritt

Harvard Business Review on Breakthrough Thinking . . . . Harvard Business School Press

Heart of the Mind . . . . Connierae Andreas & Steve Andreas

Historical Survey of Christian Education . . . . Simon S. Laurie

History of Education, A (1886) . . . . F.V.N. Painter

History of Knowledge, A . . . . Charles Van Doren

Horace Mann: Educator, Patriot and Reformer . . . . George Hubbell

How Did Sports Begin? . . . . Rudolph Brasch

How People Learn: Brain, Mind, Experience and School . . . . National Research Council

How the Mind Works . . . . Steven Pinker

How to Change the Games Children Play . . . . G. S. Don Morris

How to Teach So Students Remember (2005) . . . . Marilee Sprenger

How to Think Like Leonardo da Vinci: Seven Steps to Genius Every Day . . . . . Michael L. Gelb

I Won't Learn from You . . . . Herbert Kohl

Ideas and Opinions . . . . Albert Einstein

Illusions: The Adventures of a Reluctant Messiah . . . . Richard Bach

In Every Kid There Lurks a Tiger . . . . Rudy Duran with Rick Lipsey

Inner Game of Tennis, The . . . . W. Timothy Gallwey

Inner Game of Work, The (2000) . . . . W. Timothy Gallwey

Inside the Brain: Revolutionary Discoveries of How the Mind Works . . . . Ronald Kotulak

Insights of Genius: Imagery and Creativity in Science and Art (2000) . . . . Arthur Miller

Instant Rapport . . . . Michael Brooks

Intelligence in the Modern World: John Dewey's Philosophy (1939) . . . . Joseph Ratner

In the Zone . . . . Rhea White & Michael Murphy

Introduction to Piaget, An . . . . P. G. Richmond

Inventing Better Schools . . . . Phillip C. Schlechty

Journey to Wisdom, The . . . . Paul Olson

Journey Without Goal (1981) . . . . Chogyam Trungpa

Juicing for Life. . . . . Cherie Calbom & Maureen Keane

Keeping Mozart in Mind. . . . . Gordon L. Shaw, Ph.D.

Key to Understanding U.S. History, The. . . . . Killoran, Zimmer & Jarrett

Last Days of Socrates, The (1954). . . . . .Translated by Hugh Tredennick

Learning Brain, The (2005) . . . . Sarah Jayne Blakemore & Uta Frith

Learning Gap, The (1992). . . . . Harold Stevenson & James Stigler

Learning to Teach, Teaching to Learn: A Holistic Approach . . . . .Doug Bryan

Leonardo: The First Scientist . . . . Michael White

Life We are Given, The. . . . . George Leonard & Michael Murphy

Made to Stick (2007). . . . . Chip & Dan Heath

Magical Child . . . . .Joseph Chilton Pearce

Mapping Human History . . . . .Steve Olson

Mastery: The Keys to Success and Long-Term Fulfillment . . . . George Leonard

Memory 101 for Educators . . . . .Marilee Sprenger

Mindfulness . . . . Dr. Ellen Langer

Mindstorms: Children, computers, and Powerful Ideas . . . . Seymour Papert

Mother Tongue, The . . . . Bill Bryson

Multiple Intelligences . . . . Howard Gardner

Myself: A Case of Mistaken Identity. . . . . Alan Watts

Next: The Coming Era in Science . . . . .Holcomb B. Noble

No Quick Fix. . . . . Richard L. Allington & Sean A. Walmsley

Observations. . . . . Arthur Morgan

On Education . . . . Immanuel Kant

On Intelligence (2004). . . . . Jeff Hawkins & Sandra Blakeslee

On The Sea Of Memory . . . . Jonathan Cott

Origin of Species, The (1861) . . . . .Charles Darwin

Origins and Growth of Modern Education, The . . . . . *Elizabeth Lawrence*

Origins of Intelligence in Children, The . . . . . Jean Piaget

Out of My Later Years (1950) . . . . . Albert Einstein

Overcoming Dyslexia . . . . . Sally Shaywitz, M.D.

Owners Manual For the Brain, The . . . . . Pierce J. Howard, Ph.D.

Peak Learning (1991) . . . . . Ronald Gross

Peak Performance: Mental Training Techniques of the World's Greatest Athletes . Charles Garfield

Perfect Health . . . . . Deepak Chopra

Piaget for Teachers . . . . . Hans Furth

Piaget in the Classroom . . . . . Milton Schwebel & Jane Raph

Power of Intention, The (2004) . . . . . Dr. Wayne W. Dyer

Power of Mindful Learning, The . . . . . Dr. Ellen J. Langer

Power of Now, The . . . . . Eckhart Tolle

Pressured Child, The . . . . . Michael Thompson & Teresa Barker

Productive Learning (2007) . . . . . Stanislaw Gtazek & Seymour Sarason

Professor's Duties, A . . . . . Peter Markie

Promoting Active Learning . . . . . Chet Meyers & Thomas B. Jones

Psychology of Learning, The . . . . . Robert Borger & E. M. Seaborne

Psychology of Play, The . . . . . Susanna Millar

Quality School Teacher , The . . . . . William Glasser, M.D.

Quality School, The . . . . . William Glasser M.D.

Quotable Teacher, The . . . . . Randy Howe

Red Pencil, The . . . . . Theodore R. Sizer

Rediscovering Hope . . . . . Richard Curwin

Reframing: NLP and the Transformation of Meaning . . . . . Richard Bandler & John Grinder

Rethinking Golf . . . . . Chuck Hogan

Dr. Dean Ornish's Program for Reversing Heart Disease . . . . . Dr. Dean Ornish

Run Your Brain for a Change . . . . . Richard Bandler, Connirae Andreas & Steve Andreas

Seat of the Soul, The . . . . Gary Zukav

Secrets of Life, The. . . . . Stuart Wilde

Seven Sins of Memory, The . . . . Michael J. Gelb

Short History of Nearly Everything, A. . . . . Bill Bryson

Smart Moves: Why Learning is Not all in Your Head . . . . Dr. Carla Hannford

Smart Schools (1992) . . . . .David Perkins

Society of Mind, The . . . . Marvin Minsky

Space, Time and Beyond . . . . .Bob Toben & Fred Alan Wolf

Story of Stupidity, The . . . . .James F. Welles, Ph.D.

Sweet Spot in Time, The . . . . John Jerome

Switching On. . . . . Dr. Paul E. Dennison

Synaptic Self, The: How the Brain Becomes Who We Are . . . . Joseph Le Doux

Talks to Teachers . . . . William James

Tao of Pooh, The . . . . Benjamin Hoff

Teacher Man: A Memoir. . . . . .Frank McCourt

Teacher Speaks, A . . . . Philip Marson

Teaching as Learning . . . . Clark Moustakas

Teaching To The Brain's Natural Learning Systems. . . . . .Barbara K. Given

Teaching with Fire (2003) . . . . Sam Intrator & Megan Scribner

Teaching with the Brain in Mind. . . . . Eric Jensen

Thinker's Journal for College Freshmen, A . . . . Judy Daniel

Thinking for a Change (1989) . . . . John C. Maxwell

Tiger's Bond Of Power. . . . . Chuck Hogan

To Know as We Are Known: Education as a Spiritual Journey (1993) . . . . Parker Palmer

Touching Peace . . . . Thich Nhat Hanh

Toward a Theory of Instruction . . . . Jerome Bruner

Trance-Formations. . . . . John Grinder & Richard Bandler

Understanding Creativity (2004) . . . . .Jane Piirto, Ph.D.

Understanding How Students Learn (2006) . . . . P. Karen Murphy & Patricia A. Alexander

Understanding Waldorf Education: Teaching from the Inside Out . . . . Jack Petrash

Unschooled Mind, The . . . . Howard Gardner

Vital Lies, Simple Truths . . . . Daniel Goleman

What Does it Mean to be Well Educated? . . . . Alfie Kohn

What Great Teachers Do Differently (2004) . . . . Todd Whitaker

What is Philosophy? . . . . Gilles Deleuze & Felix Guattari

Who are You? 101 Ways of Seeing Yourself . . . . Malcolm Godwin

Why Choose this Book? (2006) . . . . Read Montague

Working Knowledge . . . . . Thomas R. Bailey, Katherine L. Hughes & David Thornton Moore

Working with Emotional Intelligence . . . . Daniel Goleman

World Perspectives in Education (1900) . . . . Edmund J. King

Magazines & Journals

American Educator (Quarterly)

International Journal of Sports, Science and Teaching

Scientific American (Magazine)

Scientific American Mind (Magazine)

About Michael Hebron

Decades ago, Michael Hebron played a key role in orchestrating the original PGA Teaching and Coaching Seminar, bringing together instructors from across the country to share ideas on teaching methods. Following that momentous event, Michael gained the nickname of "the teacher's teacher."

Highly respected throughout the international golf community, Michael consults on golf instruction to PGA Switzerland, Italy, France, Finland, Canada, Japan, and Sweden. He has given instruction clinics at 30 PGA of America sections. Through his dedication, Michael earned the honored status of becoming the 24th PGA of America Master Professional.

His book, *See and Feel the Inside Move the Outside*, was the first golf instruction book accepted as a PGA Master's thesis. Since then, he has written hundreds of articles for leading golf magazines and authored four other books and three DVDs. (See list)

He has appeared on "The Charlie Rose Show," "The Today Show," The Golf Channel, and several local cable shows.

From their very first listings, *Golf Magazine* and *Golf Digest* have consistently named Hebron as a member of America's Top 50 Instructors.

Over the years, Hebron has worked with many successful golfers from the PGA and LPGA tours and several national champions in America and abroad, including three men who each subsequently won a major tournament. He has also worked with many successful high school and college golfers - but Michael's pride is working with club golfers.

BOOKS

See and Feel the Inside Move the Outside
Building and Improving your Golf Mind, Golf Body, Golf Swing
The Art and Zen of Learning Golf
Golf Swing Secrets and Lies — Six Timeless Lessons

DVDs

Building and Improving your Golf Mind, Golf Body, Golf Swing
Blueprints for Parents and Children Learning Golf
(includes French translation)
Blueprints for Building your Golf Swing

Lightning Source UK Ltd.
Milton Keynes UK
UKOW04f1836230215

246765UK00001B/178/P